Reading Through History Presents:
History Brief:
African Americans

A Condensed History of
a Resilient People

Jake Henderson

History Brief: African Americans
A Condensed History of a Resilient People
By Jake Henderson
©2016
ISBN-13: 9781533136879

Table of Contents:

Part One: Early History, Slavery, Abolition, and Emancipation

Part Two: The Reconstruction Era, Jim Crow, and More

Part Three: The Great Migration, The Harlem Renaissance, Jazz, and Amazing Athletes

Part Four: The Civil Rights Movement

Part Four: The Civil Rights Movement
(continued)

Part Five: Modern Political Figures

Part Six: Modern Entertainment

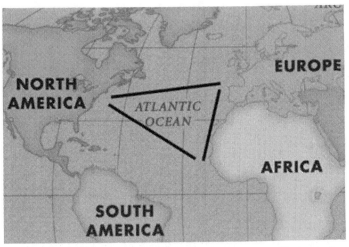

Triangular Trade brought Africans to North America, to be used as slaves. In turn, this slave-labor was used to produce molasses, sugar, rum, tobacco, and hemp which was sold in Europe. Then, products such as guns, ammunition, and cloth were taken from Europe to Africa, in exchange for more slaves.

Triangular Trade & The Middle Passage

From the 1500s through the 1800s, millions of African slaves arrived in North America via the process known as triangular trade. What was triangular trade? What role did the Middle Passage play in this process?

Triangular trade is a system of trade which mutually benefits three different locations. The most well-known example of triangular trade is that which existed between Europe, the Americas, and Africa from the 16th Century up through the 19th Century.

Ships would depart from Europe and arrive in Africa with guns, ammunition, cloth, copper, and other manufactured goods. These items would be traded to African tribal chiefs in exchange for slaves. The slaves would then be loaded onto ships and taken to the Americas. The slaves would be traded for molasses, sugar, rum, tobacco, hemp, and other cash crops that were produced by use of slave labor. These goods would be taken to Europe and sold. Revenue from these sales was used to purchase items that could be exchanged for more slaves in Africa. This cycle repeated itself thousands of times over the course of three hundred years.

The second portion of this trade route, the journey that brought Africans from their native continent to the Americas, became known as the Middle Passage. African kings, warlords, and chiefs would capture other Africans from opposing tribes. They would then exchange these captives for guns, ammunition, cloth, and other goods. The future slaves would be loaded onto boats and shipped out for the Americas.

The ships were almost always overcrowded, and captives received only small amounts of food and water (usually one meal a day). Due to the deplorable living conditions and close quarters, diseases were common. Outbreaks of smallpox, syphilis, and measles spread quickly. Starvation, poor nutrition, and lack of drinkable water also led to conditions such as dysentery and scurvy.

Many captives did not survive the journey. Some died from disease, some died due to starvation, and many simply lost the will to live and jumped overboard (or perhaps jumped in the hopes of escaping). Bodies of the departed were thrown into the sea. These deaths were so common that the routes of the ships altered the migration paths of sharks because the animals knew there would be a plentiful supply of food in the area.

Not all slaves came to the Americas peacefully. There were many reported cases of attempted uprisings amongst the captives as they tried to overthrow the crew of the ship. These mutinies were rarely successful. In 1839, slaves aboard the *Amistad* were able to gain control of their ship just off the coast of Cuba. This highly-publicized incident became influential in the Abolitionist Movement in the United States. However, most slave-uprisings aboard ship did not succeed. Those who started the uprising were apprehended and eliminated to serve as an example to the others.

Upon arriving in the Americas, the captives would be sold as slaves, either in Brazil, on an island in the Caribbean, or in the southeastern portion of what is today the United States. It has been estimated that somewhere between 9 million to 12 million Africans arrived in the Americas via the Middle Passage.

African Americans in the Revolution

There were many notable African Americans that played a role during the American Revolution. Who were these figures? What did they do?

Before the war even started, African Americans were making their presence known. During the riot which led to the Boston Massacre, colonists began pelting British soldiers with chunks of ice and snowballs. Someone in the crowd struck a soldier with a club, sending him to the snowy ground. The man sprang to his feet and was struck a second time. He raised his musket and pulled the trigger.

The other soldiers took it as a signal and fired into the crowd. A great screech came from the mob as bullets cut their way through. Crispus Attucks, a mulatto of Native American and African descent, and four other Bostonians fell dead, while six more were wounded. The mob fled in all directions. Attucks became one of the first Americans to die for the cause of

Crispus Attucks became one of the first Americans to die for the cause of American independence.

independence.

In 1776, the authors of the Declaration of Independence compared living under British rule to living as an enslaved people, but the document did not recognize the rights of enslaved African Americans. When the war began, slavery was legal in all thirteen colonies. Yet, just as white soldiers signed up to fight for the Revolutionary cause, as many as 5,000 African Americans did so as well.

At the beginning of the war, one in six colonists was African American, and of those, 99% were slaves. Most lived in the Southern colonies, but New York and New Jersey also had large slave populations. When the Revolution began, African Americans reacted with hope and excitement. Many were equally ecstatic about the words of the Declaration of Independence which declared that "all men are created equal."

As the war escalated, African Americans faced many tough choices about which side to support. In Virginia, the royal governor offered freedom to any slave who deserted their master and signed up to fight for the British Army. While this policy was temporarily dropped by the British because it alienated many wealthy loyalists in the South, it became a full, military-wide policy 1779. Sir Henry Clinton, the supreme British commander at the time of the implementation, argued that the policy was justified because the Continental Army was using African American soldiers as well.

After initial hesitation due to Southern objections,

free African Americans were accepted into the Continental Army. By 1779, a full 15% of Washington's army was African American.

Rhode Island was the first state to field an all African American unit in 1777. Massachusetts chose to mix black and white soldiers together. Every colony, with the exception of South Carolina, enlisted free African Americans to fight. However, not all black Americans who fought for the Patriot cause did so of their own choosing. When the states began drafting militiamen into full military service, many Southerners sent slaves in their place, offering them freedom if they served honorably.

In the final stages of the war, the British shifted their focus to the Southern colonies where a substantial number of loyalists and slaves provided manpower and support to their armies. As the brutality of the war intensified, many British officers began viewing runaway slaves as contraband (goods to be seized and confiscated). Sadly, thousands were sold into an even worse form of slavery in the West Indies, with greedy British officers making as much as $1,000 for each slave they sold.

In spite of the arguments and turmoil, the service of African Americans changed the minds of many white Americans. By the end of the war, Vermont, Massachusetts, and New Hampshire had abolished slavery. Pennsylvania, Rhode Island, and Connecticut also voted in plans to gradually do away with the institution.
In Boston, Phillis Wheatley, a talented African Ameri-

can author whose writing was often supportive of the Patriot cause, celebrated the end of the war and her freedom with a poem entitled "Liberty and Peace."

"Auspicious Heaven shall fill with fav'ring Gales,
Where e'er Columbia spreads her swelling Sails:
To every Realm shall Peace her Charms display,
And Heavenly Freedom spread her golden Ray."

The Slave Codes & Nat Turner's Rebellion

In 1831, Nat Turner led a slave rebellion in Virginia. Who was Nat Turner? What was the outcome of that rebellion?

Throughout the colonial era of American history, as well as the early history of the United States, laws known as slave codes were in place. The slave codes were laws which established the status of slaves in society, as well as the rights that owners had in regards to those slaves.

The slave codes varied from state to state, but many of the laws were quite similar. For example, most states had a law regarding how it was determined whether someone was, or was not a slave. Generally, it was ruled that "the child followed the condition of the mother". This meant that if the mother was a slave, then the child was also a slave. If the mother was free, then the child would be free as well.

Other laws regarded abuse between master and

slave. A Virginia law from 1705 stated that if a master killed his slave while in the process of punishing him, the master would be free of punishment. Meanwhile, a Louisiana law from 1724 stated if a slave struck his master hard enough to produce a bruise or draw blood, then death was an appropriate punishment.

In some states, slaves were forbidden from leaving their owner's property without being accompanied by a white person. Additionally, any slave caught attempting to run away could be subjected to the death penalty. Slaves were also prohibited from possessing weapons.

Punishments for violating the slave codes could be severe. These punishments could include, but were not limited to, public whippings. Runaway slaves might have an R branded on their right cheek or could have an ear cut off. These punishments served as an example to other slaves that they should not attempt the same thing.

The slave codes also had provisions for those who attempted to help slaves. An Alabama law made it illegal to teach slaves how to read, spell, or write. Anyone caught violating this law would be fined somewhere in between $250 to $500. Someone caught trying to harbor runaway slaves could be fined up to $1,000 or incarcerated for a year.

It was the harsh nature and severity of the slave codes that eventually prompted Nat Turner to take action. Turner was born a slave on October 2, 1800. He lived in Southampton County, Virginia. At a young age, he became deeply religious and preached to his fellow slaves who called him "The Prophet". He earned this nickname because he claimed to have visions which he believed were messages from God. He became convinced that God had instructed him to slay his enemies with their own weapons.

Turner began planning a rebellion against slave owners. He recruited the assistance of other slaves, and they began orchestrating their efforts to revolt. On August 21st, 1831, he and his followers began their uprising.

They moved from house to house, using knives, axes, hatchets, and other blunt objects to attack those inside. The group killed indiscriminately, murdering men, women, and children. The only homes that were spared were those of poor whites.

The rebellion only lasted two days, but before they could be stopped, Turner and his followers killed sixty people. Fifty-six suspects were apprehended and executed for their participation in the revolt. White mobs also killed another two hundred blacks, simply out of fear and hysteria.

Nat Turner eluded capture for more than two months. He was eventually captured and placed on trial for "conspiring to rebel and making insurrection". He was found guilty and sentenced to death. He was hanged on November 11, 1831. After his hanging, his body was then skinned, beheaded, and quartered.

Turner remains a controversial figure to this day. Some view him as a hero for standing up against slav-

Nat Turner led a save rebellion in Virginia, in 1831.

ery. They claim he made slave owners suffer for the hardships they had inflicted upon so many. Others argue that Turner was a blood-thirsty fanatic. They suggest that the murder of women and children, done at his command, is inexcusable and unforgivable.

A Day in the Life of a Slave

Most people would agree that slaves lived a difficult life, but just how difficult was it? What was the day to day life of a slave really like?

The average African American slave lived on a plantation in the Southern United States. Plantations usually had at least 20 slaves, however, some of the larger ones had as many as 500!

Most slaves lived in an area known as "the quarters". These were rows of small huts that were usually about 16 feet by 16 feet. These structures commonly had no floor (except the ground) and often did not have a window.

Ten to twelve people usually lived in each of these structures. They slept on the ground and were given only a small, filthy blanket to sleep on or under.

Slaves were woken at sunrise. After that, they went to work the fields or pick cotton *all day long*. Cotton was a difficult crop to pick because it contains thistles which could easily damage the skin while picking. They would continue working until dark, at which time, if they had not picked their quota, they would be punished.

After dark, they could then make their evening meal, wash their clothes, and do anything else they needed to do before going to sleep to repeat the process the next day.

Most owners gave their slaves a monthly allowance of food. On average, each slave was given eight pounds of pork and one bushel of cornmeal to last an entire month. Some owners allowed slaves to keep small gardens for growing vegetables.

Each year, the average slave would receive two shirts, one pair of pants, a pair of socks, and a pair of shoes. These were typically given as Christmas presents and had to last the entire year (meaning if a child outgrew the shirt, pants, or shoes, he/she would have to do without until the next Christmas).

If a slave did something their owner thought was wrong, the slave was punished. The most common form of punishment was whipping. Ten to fifteen lashes were common, but sometimes it could be many more. Other forms of punishment were used as well. By far, the worst form of punishment was death. Some owners were known to kill slaves that they were especially unhappy with.

It should be noted that every slave had a different experience. Some owners were horrible towards their slaves; however, some treated their slaves very well.

Regardless of treatment, we can be certain that almost no one wanted to be enslaved and forced to do someone else's bidding.

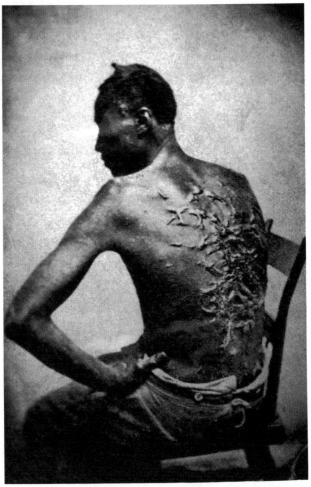

This image shows scars on the back of a slave who has been whipped.

Harriet Tubman

Harriet Tubman is remembered today as one of the most legendary figures of the anti-slavery movement. Who was Harriet Tubman, and how did she become so well-known?

Harriet Tubman was born a slave around 1820, although, no one truly knows the exact date of her birth. She was the fifth of nine children and lived a difficult life in her early years (as most slaves did).

One day, as a youth, she was sent to the store to purchase supplies. While she was out, she encountered a runaway slave. The slave's overseer (who was attempting to apprehend him) demanded that Harriet assist in restraining the man, but she refused. The overseer picked up a two pound weight, attempting to throw it at the runaway. However, he missed and struck Harriet in the back of the head. She returned home, bleeding, where she eventually passed out. She was sent back to work in the fields, receiving no medical treatment. This incident caused her to suffer from seizures for the rest of her life, and she would fre-

Harriet Tubman

quently fall into a deep sleep without warning.

In 1849, Harriet and two of her brothers made their first attempt at escaping, but the brothers panicked, and the group was forced to return. Not long after that, Harriet made a second attempt and was able to escape slavery for good.

To make her journey to freedom, she utilized the Underground Railroad, which was a series of destination points and hiding places, organized by different abolitionists (those who opposed slavery). Following her escape, she would go on to become the most well-known "conductor" on this Underground Railroad.

On at least nineteen separate occasions, she risked her life making repeated trips into the South, leading slaves to freedom. Each trip was increasingly dangerous because she risked losing her own freedom as well (she also had several large rewards posted for her capture).

Helping slaves escape was not an easy task. Her journeys were filled with peril and could potentially be life-threatening for all involved. It required courage, the ability to think (and stay calm) under pressure, and a lot of ingenuity.

She typically worked in the winter, when the nights were longer and most people hoped to stay out of the cold. She usually met her escaping family on a Saturday evening. This allowed for the maximum escape time, before "runaway notices" could be printed in Monday's newspaper.

If a slave agreed to escape with her, there was no

turning back. She informed them that if they attempted to return, she would shoot them rather than risk
others getting caught. Though she made the threat
many times, and did carry a gun, she never once had
to carry out this threat.

She used many ingenious tactics to avoid being de-
tected. Once, she brought along a chicken tied to a
string, and when she saw an approaching overseer, she
turned the chicken loose and pretended to chase the
animal as it "escaped" into a cornfield.

On another occasion, she spotted a man that she
knew was chasing her. She quickly grabbed a newspaper and pretended to read. Since it was well-known
that Tubman was illiterate, the man passed her by
without notice.

On yet another trip, she and her "passengers" were
being pursued by slave catchers at a train station. The
slave catchers were only searching northbound trains,
so she and her passengers boarded a southbound
train, taking them deeper into the South. The ruse
worked, and she and her fellow travelers were never
discovered.

She continued leading slaves to freedom throughout the 1850s. Slave owners made many efforts and
offered large rewards in hopes of catching her, but
never could. In her later years, while being asked to
reflect on her heroic journeys, Tubman smiled as she
stated, "I never lost a single passenger."

Over the course of eleven years, she led around 300
people from the bonds of slavery, while aiding in the

liberation of hundreds of others. She became so well-known and revered, that she earned herself the nick-name "The Moses of Her People" (named after the Biblical Moses who led the Israelites from slavery in Egypt).

During the Civil War, she served her country in numerous capacities, from providing care to wounded soldiers and even entering Confederate camps to act as a spy! Most notably, she guided Union soldiers through the Southern wilderness that she had learned so well during her years of helping runaway slaves.

After the war, Tubman became involved in the women's suffrage movement. She traveled to major cities and spoke to gatherings about the issue. She was also the keynote speaker at the first meeting of the National Federation of Afro-American Women in 1896.

In her later years, she was bothered more and more by her childhood injury, even resorting to brain surgery in an attempt to relieve some of the symptoms. In 1911, she was admitted into a rest home (which was named after her) and lived out the remaining years of her life. She died in 1913 of pneumonia.

After her death, she became a legendary figure, remembered with the same reverence as Paul Revere and Betsy Ross. There have been countless tributes, schools named in her honor, and in 1978, the United States Postal Service honored her with a stamp as part of a series featuring important African Americans.

More importantly though, she served as an inspiration for African Americans as they strived and struggled for civil rights throughout the 20th Century.

This picture of Tubman was taken in about 1885

The Underground Railroad

In the mid-1800s, thousands of slaves escaped the shackles of slavery using the Underground Railroad. What was the Underground Railroad? Why was it called that?

In 1834, slavery was abolished in Canada. From that point on, Canada became the main destination point for slaves attempting to escape. Several hundred slaves would escape each year, and as time went by, that number progressively increased.

As more slaves escaped, and the Abolitionist Movement in the Northern states continued to grow, there was an expanding need for a network of people to assist fugitive slaves.

Abolitionists, free blacks, former slaves, Native Americans, and various religious groups (such as the Quakers) helped the escaping slaves in any way they could. From providing food, offering shelter, transportation, or other forms of assistance, these people helped to create what would eventually be known as the Underground Railroad.

The Underground Railroad was not underground at all. It was referred to as "underground" because it was supposed to be hidden. Strong efforts were made to keep everything secret. Escape routes were only known by a select few, most information was only passed by word of mouth, and, in many cases, a participant might only know their part of the operation.

The Underground Railroad was not a railroad either. It was referred to as a "railroad" because those who operated it used railroad terminology as code words. For example, the one in charge of leading the slaves to freedom was a "conductor". Harriet Tubman, the most famous conductor, personally led more than 300 slaves to freedom over the course of a decade.

This image is titled "A Ride for Liberty" and depicts fugitive slaves making their escape to freedom.

Escaping slaves were known as "passengers", and the hiding places and rest stops were called "train stations" or "depots". Also, the owner of a hiding spot might be called a "station master", and anyone supporting the cause with food or money was referred to as a "stockholder".

There was great risk involved in the Underground Railroad. Obviously, the escaping slaves were at risk of being caught. However, they were not the only ones at risk. Conductors were usually former slaves who risked being captured, or even executed, for helping others escape.

Whites who harbored runaways risked heavy fines, or even jail time if caught. Especially after the passage of the Fugitive Slave Act of 1850 which required anyone, even those living in non-slave states, to help slave owners catch runaway slaves.

No one is certain how many slaves escaped via the Underground Railroad. Estimates suggest anywhere from 6,000 all the way up to 100,000 slaves made their way north and into Canada.

The Fugitive Slave Act of 1850

The Fugitive Slave Act of 1850 was one of the most controversial laws ever passed. What was the Fugitive Slave Act? Why was it enacted?

In 1793, Congress passed a law which stated that all fugitive slaves (runaways) had to be returned to their masters. While it was enforced after it was passed, as time went by, many people in the Northern states (where slavery was illegal) began ignoring the law.

In fact, many Northerners did everything they could to circumvent the old Fugitive Slave Act, helping slaves run away and escape into Canada. It was this refusal to enforce the old law that prompted Southern slave owners to desire a new law. This led to the Fugitive Slave Act of 1850.

The act was part of a larger package of five bills known as the Compromise of 1850. The Compromise of 1850 was an agreement made between Northern legislators and Southern congressmen in which they

This poster warned African Americans of Boston of some of the provisions laid out in the Fugitive Slave Act of 1850.

each gave up something they desired in order to avoid conflict. This agreement, which had been orchestrated by the legendary Senator Henry Clay, helped to avoid civil war for several years.

The Fugitive Slave Act was one of the principle parts of the compromise. It stated that all fugitive slaves must be returned to their masters. It also stated that any law enforcement official who did not assist with the return of a runaway would be fined $1,000 (that would be over $25,000 today!)

According to the law, even an African American who was *suspected* of being a fugitive slave could be apprehended. Once arrested, the suspected runaway had no right to a trial (because slaves and most free blacks were not considered full citizens). Police officers, and other law enforcement officials, who arrested runaways would be given a pay bonus for their work (this gave them a reason to arrest anyone who looked like they might be an escaping slave).

Additionally, any person who was caught giving shelter, food, or protection to a runaway slave could be subject to up to six months in prison.

The Fugitive Slave Act of 1850 infuriated Northerners. They felt that obligating Northern law enforcement agents to enforce this law was an underhanded method of expanding the power and reach of slavery. Congress had made it illegal to even assist a fugitive slave, and offering bonuses to law enforcement officials who caught suspected runaways made it dangerous for free blacks everywhere—not just in the South.

While the Fugitive Slave Act, as well as the other provisions in the Compromise of 1850, was supposed to diffuse tensions, it only succeeded in making things worse. As the 1850s progressed, and resentment towards the new law grew, it drove the two sides closer and closer to civil war.

The Dred Scott Decision

The Dred Scott Decision is one of the most famous Supreme Court decisions ever. Who was Dred Scott? What was his court case about?

Dred Scott was a slave born in Virginia. After being sold to a man named Dr. John Emerson, the new owner took him to Illinois. Illinois was a free state, meaning slavery was illegal there. At that point, Scott could have sued for his freedom, but he was unaware of the law.

In 1836, Emerson took him even further north into Wisconsin Territory where slavery was illegal as well. While in Wisconsin, Dr. Emerson rented Scott out to others. This was a severe violation of the law (he was actively spreading the institution of slavery into a free territory).

Emerson eventually moved to the South, bringing Dred Scott and his wife with him. During the journey, Scott's wife gave birth to their daughter. Since she was

Dred Scott

born in a free territory, she should have been a free person, but again, Scott was unaware of the law.

Finally, in 1846, Scott sued for his family's freedom. The case went to court where Scott lost the initial decision, but he appealed to a higher court. They won the appeal, but the decision was challenged yet again.

The appeals process lasted so long that the trials outlived Dr. Emerson! Scott's ownership was passed to his wife's brother, John Sanford.

Finally, after over ten years, the case of *Scott v. Sanford* reached the Supreme Court. The court's 1857 ruling stated that Dred Scott, a slave, was not a citizen of the United States and therefore had no right to have a case heard in a federal court. The decision also concluded that slaves fell under 5th Amendment property rights and that Congress had no power to take citizens' property away. Thus, the court concluded, the Missouri Compromise, prohibiting slavery north of the 36°30' parallel, was unconstitutional, and slaves, as property, should be able to be taken anywhere inside of U.S. territories.

Chief Justice Roger Taney felt that the Dred Scott Decision would settle the issue of slavery once and for all. However, it had the exact opposite result. Those who opposed slavery were furious about the decision. They saw it as an effort to broaden the reach of slavery.

As for Dred Scott, despite losing his case, he and his family did eventually gain their freedom. The sons of his original owner (Peter Blow) purchased emancipation for Scott, his wife, and their daughter. He lived out the rest of his life as a free man working in a hotel in St. Louis, Missouri.

The Dred Scott Decision is remembered as one of the most controversial decisions ever made by the Supreme Court. As the United States moved into the late 1850s, it was one of the major events that pushed the nation ever closer to the Civil War.

UNCLE TOM'S CABIN;

OR,

LIFE AMONG THE LOWLY.

BY

HARRIET BEECHER STOWE.

VOL. I.

ONE HUNDRED AND FIFTH THOUSAND.

BOSTON:

JOHN P. JEWETT & COMPANY

CLEVELAND, OHIO:

JEWETT, PROCTOR & WORTHINGTON.

1852.

Uncle Tom's Cabin

One of the most influential novels of the 1800s was Uncle Tom's Cabin. Why was this book so important? Just how popular was it?

In June of 1851, an abolitionist newspaper called *National Era* published the first of what would eventually be a 40-week-long serial. The story became so popular that the newspaper's editor convinced the author to publish the series as a full-length novel. The author's name was Harriet Beecher Stowe, and her novel was titled *Uncle Tom's Cabin.*

The book relays the story of several slaves, including Tom, and their owners. One central character, a slave woman named Eliza, learns that her son is about to be sold to a slave trader. Rather than lose her only son, she decides to run away with him. As the tale unfolds, the reader begins to understand how the lives of slaves and owners were interconnected. The major themes of the story include the corrupting nature of slavery and how the institution divided and destroyed families.

As soon as it was published, *Uncle Tom's Cabin* was instantly successful. It sold over 300,000 copies in its first year. The book was lauded by abolitionists who praised it for exposing the evils of slavery. However, Southerners were outraged, claiming the book had no basis in fact.

The novel was overwhelmingly persuasive, helping to fuel the momentum of the abolitionist cause in the 1850s. It has even been credited by many historians for helping to lay the groundwork for the American Civil War.

Not long after its publication, a live theatrical version of *Uncle Tom's Cabin* began touring the country. Other than the names of the central characters, this live version had little in common with the book, but it became equally influential (if not more so). For comparison, it is estimated that nearly ten times as many people saw the play as read the book. Different stage versions of the story continued to be performed throughout the 1800s and even well into the 20th Century.

As for the novel, its popularity continued to grow, especially during the years of the Civil War. It was translated into no less than twenty languages, including Chinese! It was the best-selling novel of the 19th Century, and for a brief time, it outsold every other book except the Bible.

The Abolitionists

In the years leading up to the Civil War, abolition-ists encouraged an end to the institution of slavery. Who were the abolitionists? How big was the move-ment?

Abolitionists were those who opposed slavery. They did so for many reasons. Some saw how slavery tore families apart. Others saw how the institution corrupted many owners who were otherwise good people. Still others saw the religious and moral impli-cations of holding another against their will. However, regardless of their reasons, they all saw slavery for the evil abomination that it was.

The leader of the abolitionist movement in the United States was William Lloyd Garrison. Garrison founded the American Anti-Slavery Society and pub-lished an anti-slavery newspaper known as *The Liber-ator*. *The Liberator* had a very small circulation, nev-er reaching more than about 3,000 subscribers. How-

William Lloyd Garrison

ever, there were undoubtedly many people who read *The Liberator* regularly, but were not subscribers. Its influence was widespread throughout the 1840s and 50s.

Some involved in the abolitionist movement were former slaves. The most prominent of these was Frederick Douglass. Douglass was an eloquent writer and speaker who had a newspaper of his own called *The North Star*. Sojourner Truth and Harriet Tubman were also former slaves who appeared at events around the country to speak on the evils of slavery.

Other women were also involved in the Abolitionist Movement. One of the most notable was Harriet Beecher Stowe. Her novel, *Uncle Tom's Cabin*, became one of the most influential pieces of anti-slavery literature in the 1850s.

Two other women who played an important role were the Grimké sisters. Angelina and Sara Grimké were Southerners who grew to see slavery for what it was. After moving north, they wrote several anti-slavery pamphlets and toured the nation speaking to different audiences. Being Southerners, their perspective was valued by many people.

Most abolitionists were peaceful and worked to abolish slavery through speeches and writings. But some thought the best way to end slavery would be through violence. This view is best displayed through an aggressive abolitionist named John Brown. In 1859, he and over 20 others seized a federal armory in Harper's Ferry, Virginia. They believed that their actions would cause a massive slave revolt. This did not happen, and Brown was captured. He was tried for treason and hanged.

The American abolitionist came in many different forms. However, whether they were wealthy white men, former slaves, women, or violent activists, they all shared one goal. They all hoped to bring an end to the institution of slavery.

Frederick Douglass

Frederick Douglass was one of the key figures of the abolitionist movement. Who was Frederick Douglass? Why is he important today?

Douglass was born and raised as a slave in Maryland. He was separated from his family when he was seven and was transferred from one owner to another, before ending up in the home of Hugh Auld. Auld's wife, Sophie, was influential in Frederick's life, for she taught him the basic skills of reading. Teaching slaves to read was highly discouraged—in fact, it was even illegal!

Douglass continued to teach himself how to read and write, in secret, and started reading everything he could find. The books, newspapers, and pamphlets he read, led him to think about slavery in new ways, and he began to understand how deplorable it really was. This was exactly why many owners did not want slaves to learn how to read. They feared that if slaves could read, they would begin to want more freedom.

Eventually, he began to teach other slaves to read. They would come and learn from him on a weekly basis. While Douglass' owner saw no harm in the weekly sessions, others did not want their slaves taught by him. So, one Sunday, the owners broke up the meeting using clubs and rocks, and the group never met again.

Frederick eventually did try to seek his freedom. He attempted to escape twice, and failed, before finally succeeding on his third attempt. In September of 1838, he became a free man.

After gaining his freedom, Douglass quickly became involved in the abolitionist movement. At the age of 23, he delivered his first speech about how horrible his life as a slave had been. He quickly became well-known for his eloquent speeches and his writing ability. He spoke in numerous towns across the Midwest and Northeast United States. Not everyone was a fan of what he had to say, however. He was attacked verbally, and physically at various times, including one incident where he was chased by a violent mob.

Douglass authored several books, the most notable of which is his autobiography titled *Narrative of the Life of Frederick Douglass, An American Slave*. The book was published in multiple languages, resulting in several European speaking tours. He also started his own newspaper, an anti-slavery publication known as *The North Star*.

During the Civil War, he served the Union by help-

Frederick Douglass

ing recruit soldiers for the 54th Massachusetts (a regiment made up entirely of Africa American soldiers). He also spoke with President Lincoln, regarding the treatment of black men serving in the army.

For the remainder of his life, Frederick Douglass continued to be an important figure, fighting not only for African American rights, but women's rights as well. He remained a very outspoken man until 1895, when he suffered a massive heart attack and died at his home in Washington DC. Thousands arrived at his funeral to pay tribute to this great man.

Sojourner Truth

One of the most famous African American women in history is Sojourner Truth. Who was Sojourner Truth? Why did she become so well-known?

Sojourner Truth was born with the name Isabella (Belle) Baumfree in the mid-1790s. She was raised as a slave in the state of New York. She spoke only Dutch for the first several years of her life, as it was the language spoken in the home of her first master. When she was about nine years old, she was sold, along with a flock of sheep, to a new master for $100. She was sold several more times before eventually ending up with her final master, John Dumont.

Dumont owned Belle for many years and promised to release her in 1826. However, he changed his mind, and she decided to run away rather than see her infant daughter sold away from her. However, New York abolished slavery in 1827, freeing Belle and her children from slavery forever. Following her emancipa-

Sojourner Truth

tion, she learned that one of her sons, Peter, had been illegally sold to a man in Alabama. She took the case to court and successfully sued to have her son returned to her. This made her one of the first African American women to win a court case against a white man.

In 1829, she became a devout Christian. She met a self-proclaimed prophet, Robert Matthews, and went to work for him as a housekeeper at the Matthias Kingdom Communal Colony. In 1843, she felt a spiritual calling. She changed her name to Sojourner Truth and began speaking across the country about the abolition of slavery. She chose this name because "sojourn" means to make a journey, or travel from place to place.

As Truth became a more prominent speaker, she expanded her focus to not only the abolition of slavery, but also working towards women's rights and religious tolerance. She was also a strong advocate of pacifism. In 1851, while attending the Ohio Women's Rights Convention, she delivered an extemporaneous speech which has become known in history as the "Ain't I a Woman" speech. She is reported to have said:

"Look at me! Look at my arms! I have ploughed, and planted, and reaped as much as any man! And ain't I a woman? I could work as much and eat as much as a man – and bear the lash as well! And ain't I a woman? I have borne thirteen children, and seen most of them sold into slavery, and when I cried out with my mother's grief, no one but Jesus heard me! And ain't I a woman?"

While there is no exact record of her speech, most versions include some variation of these words. It easily became her most significant speech and launched her into national prominence. (It's believed Sojourner only had five children, but this exaggeration might have been on the part of journalists of the era.)

Throughout the next several years of her life, Truth spoke in front of dozens of audiences across the country. She spoke forcefully about the evils of slavery and promoted women's suffrage (right to vote).

Sojourner Truth died in 1883, at her home in Battle Creek, Michigan. Her funeral was held in the Battle Creek Tabernacle and more than 3,000 people entered to pay their respects to this legendary woman. Since her death, she has been honored in numerous ways. There is a monument dedicated to her legacy in Battle Creek, and she has also had numerous things named in her honor, including highways, schools, and libraries.

In 1981, she was inducted into the National Women's Hall of Fame in Seneca Falls, New York. Also, in 2009, she became the first African American woman to have a bust displayed in the U.S. Capitol Building. Truth is also regarded as a saint in both the Episcopal and Lutheran churches.

The 54th Massachusetts Infantry Regiment

One of the first African American military units was the 54th Massachusetts Regiment. How did this unit come into existence? What were some of their notable accomplishments?

Following the issuance of the Emancipation Proclamation, Massachusetts Governor John A. Andrew authorized the creation of an entirely African American regiment. This regiment became known as the 54th Massachusetts Infantry Regiment. It was one of the first African American regiments created in the United States (the 1st South Carolina Volunteers had become the first in January of 1863).

The 54th Massachusetts was made up of African Americans who had volunteered to serve the United States. In fact, there were so many volunteers that they established strict physical requirements in order to serve in the regiment. They trained near Boston, Massachusetts and received much support from the

This painting is entitled "The Storming of Fort Wagner" and commemorates one of the most historic moments in the history of the 54th Massachusetts

locals, including uniforms, battle flags, other necessary supplies, and moral support as well.

The 54th Massachusetts was initially commanded by Colonel Robert Shaw, who was white. This became a standard practice for the U.S. Army that all African American units would be commanded by white officers. Upon receiving the command, Shaw felt that the attempt to create an African American regiment would fail, but he eventually grew to respect his men as outstanding soldiers.

The regiment first saw action on July 16th, 1863. That day, they helped stop a Confederate assault on James Island, South Carolina. Two days later, the regiment gained notoriety by leading an assault on Fort Wagner, not far from Charleston, South Carolina. During this battle, Colonel Shaw and twenty-nine of his men were killed (twenty-four more eventually died from wounds). The Confederacy maintained control of the fort, but the 54th was praised for its bravery during the battle.

Following the Battle of Olustee, the regiment was ordered to guard a locomotive carrying wounded Union soldiers. It had broken down and the soldiers were in danger of being captured. The men of the 54th Massachusetts used ropes to manually pull the train three miles before horses could be found. Even after horses had been secured, the soldiers continued pulling the train (with the help of the horses) for another ten miles.

Those who had joined the 54th Massachusetts had

been promised that they would receive the same pay as their white counterparts, which was $14 a month. However, they were eventually informed that their pay would only be $10 a month, and $3 of this would be withheld for clothing (white soldiers were not required to pay for their own clothing). The soldiers were insulted and outraged and boycotted their pay all together, refusing to accept the $7 a month. They even began using this as a rally cry, going into battle shouting "Massachusetts and seven dollars a month!" Finally, Congress authorized equal pay for the African American enlisted troops in September of 1864.

The legacy of the 54th Massachusetts Infantry has been remembered in a number of different ways. In the late 1800s, a monument was sculpted in their honor in Boston, Massachusetts. Additionally, various poems have been written about Colonel Shaw and his regiment. Most notable though, was a major motion picture in 1989, *Glory*, which tells the story of Colonel Shaw and the 54th Massachusetts Infantry Regiment.

The Emancipation Proclamation

One of the most important things Abraham Lin-coln did while he was president was issue the Eman-cipation Proclamation. What did the Proclamation say? Why is it so important?

The Emancipation Proclamation was issued on January 1, 1863. It was an Executive Order announc-ing that all slaves in the rebelling states were to be freed.

January 1, 1863
By the President of the United States of America:
A Proclamation.

Whereas, on the twenty-second day of September, in the year of our Lord one thousand eight hundred and sixty-two, a proclamation was issued by the President of the United States, containing, among other things, the following, to wit:

"That on the first day of January, in the year of

our Lord one thousand eight hundred and sixty-three, all persons held as slaves within any State or designated part of a State, the people whereof shall then be in rebellion against the United States, shall be then, thenceforward, and forever free; and the Executive Government of the United States, including the military and naval authority thereof, will recognize and maintain the freedom of such persons, and will do no act or acts to repress such persons, or any of them, in any efforts they may make for their actual freedom.

"That the Executive will, on the first day of January aforesaid, by proclamation, designate the States and parts of States, if any, in which the people thereof, respectively, shall then be in rebellion against the United States; and the fact that any State, or the people thereof, shall on that day be, in good faith, represented in the Congress of the United States by members chosen thereto at elections wherein a majority of the qualified voters of such State shall have participated, shall, in the absence of strong countervailing testimony, be deemed conclusive evidence that such State, and the people thereof, are not then in rebellion against the United States."

Now, therefore I, Abraham Lincoln, President of the United States, by virtue of the power in me vested as Commander-in-Chief, of the Army and Navy of the United States in time of actual armed rebellion against the authority and government of the United States, and as a fit and necessary war measure for suppressing said rebellion, do, on this first day of

January, in the year of our Lord one thousand eight hundred and sixty-three, and in accordance with my purpose so to do publicly proclaimed for the full period of one hundred days, from the day first above mentioned, order and designate as the States and parts of States wherein the people thereof respectively, are this day in rebellion against the United States, the following, to wit:

Arkansas, Texas, Louisiana, (except the Parishes of St. Bernard, Plaquemines, Jefferson, St. John, St. Charles, St. James Ascension, Assumption, Terrebonne, Lafourche, St. Mary, St. Martin, and Orleans, including the City of New Orleans) Mississippi, Alabama, Florida, Georgia, South Carolina, North Carolina, and Virginia, (except the forty-eight counties designated as West Virginia, and also the counties of Berkley, Accomac, Northampton, Elizabeth City, York, Princess Ann, and Norfolk, including the cities of Norfolk and Portsmouth[)], and which excepted parts, are for the present, left precisely as if this proclamation were not issued.

And by virtue of the power, and for the purpose aforesaid, I do order and declare that all persons held as slaves within said designated States, and parts of States, are, and henceforward shall be free; and that the Executive government of the United States, including the military and naval authorities thereof, will recognize and maintain the freedom of said persons.

And I hereby enjoin upon the people so declared to

be free to abstain from all violence, unless in necessary self-defence; and I recommend to them that, in
all cases when allowed, they labor faithfully for rea-
sonable wages.

And I further declare and make known, that such persons of suitable condition, will be received into the
armed service of the United States to garrison forts,
positions, stations, and other places, and to man ves-
sels of all sorts in said service.

And upon this act, sincerely believed to be an act of
justice, warranted by the Constitution, upon military
necessity, I invoke the considerate judgment of man-
kind, and the gracious favor of Almighty God.

In witness whereof, I have hereunto set my hand
and caused the seal of the United States to be affixed.

Done at the City of Washington, this first day of January, in the year of our Lord one thousand eight hundred and sixty three, and of the Independence of the
United States of America the eighty-seventh.

By the President: ABRAHAM LINCOLN
WILLIAM H. SEWARD, Secretary of State

The Emancipation Proclamation did not free that
many slaves at first. There were about 20,000 who
were freed as soon as they order took effect. This was
a small number compared to the 3.1 million slaves the
proclamation actually applied to. Since those slaves
lived in states that did not consider themselves to be a
part of the United States, it was difficult to enforce the
order in those areas. However, the Emancipation

*President Abraham Lincoln issued the
Emancipation Proclamation.*

Proclamation had a major impact as the war progressed.

First, the issuance of this Executive Order made slavery the key issue of the war. Prior to the Emancipation Proclamation, the primary goal of the war had always been preserving the Union. From that point forward, though, the focus of the war was abolishing slavery as well as preserving the Union. Additionally, as Union soldiers captured new areas, the slaves in those territories were immediately set free.

The Emancipation Proclamation was not entirely popular when first issued. In fact, many thought the President was overstepping his authority. However, most foreign nations applauded the effort. In fact, because of this announcement, no foreign nation would consider recognizing the Confederacy as a legitimate nation.

The 13th, 14th, and 15th Amendments

In the aftermath of the Civil War, there were three vitally important amendments passed to the United States Constitution. Which amendments were these? What did they accomplish?

While the Civil War was still being fought, the United States Senate passed an amendment to the Constitution on April 8th, 1864. On January 31st, 1865, the House of Representatives passed this same amendment. Even though the amendment had been passed by both houses of Congress, it had not become law yet.

In order to become law, it needed to be ratified by three-fourths of the states. Eighteen states ratified the new amendment almost immediately, in February of 1865. However, the proposed amendment needed twenty-seven states to become official. Georgia became the twenty-seventh state to approve the amendment, which it did on December 6th, 1865. With that, the 13th Amendment to the United States Constitution

Following the passage of the 13th Amendment, there was a great celebration amongst the members of Congress. They threw their hats in the air and cheered wildly.

officially became law on December 18th of that same year.

The 13th Amendment states:

Section 1. *Neither slavery nor involuntary servitude, except as a punishment for crime whereof the party shall have been duly convicted, shall exist within the United States, or any place subject to their jurisdiction.*

Section 2. *Congress shall have power to enforce this article by appropriate legislation.*

This amendment abolished slavery in the United States, except in cases where the labor was being used as punishment for a crime. Its impact was instantaneous. While most slaves had already been freed because of the conclusion of the Civil War, there were still anywhere from 50,000 to 100,000 slaves throughout the South who immediately became free because of the 13th Amendment.

However, even though slavery had become illegal, involuntary labor continued to be an issue throughout the South for many years. Law enforcement officials who were not enforcing the law, violence by white supremacists, and laws which restricted the freedom of African Americans (known as the Black Codes) all resulted in situations which challenged the new amendment.

Just a few years later, in 1868, another Constitutional amendment was passed. The 14th Amendment became one of the most vital, and controversial, amendments to ever be ratified. Section One of the 14th Amendment states:

Section 1. *All persons born or naturalized in the United States, and subject to the jurisdiction thereof, are citizens of the United States and of the State wherein they reside. No State shall make or enforce any law which shall abridge the privileges or immunities of citizens of the United States; nor shall any State deprive any person of life, liberty, or property, without due process of law; nor deny to any person within its jurisdiction the equal protection of the laws.*

This amendment granted citizenship to all former slaves and guaranteed equal protection under the law. This section of the amendment includes several important clauses. The first sentence is known as the Citizenship Clause, which is the clause which actually grants citizenship to former slaves. The second sentence includes both the Due Process Clause as well as the Equal Protection Clause.

The Due Process Clause states that no State shall "deprive any person of life, liberty, or property, without due process of law." This clause was cited in many Supreme Court cases throughout the 20th Century, and was used to apply every part of the Bill of Rights to state laws. This also established that there are certain rules and procedures that state laws are required to adhere to.

The Equal Protection Clause states that all those living within a state will be granted "equal protection of the laws." This means that all laws must be applied the same way to every person. The Equal Protection Clause has also been used in many Supreme Court cases, including *Brown v. the Board of Education* (1954), which successfully argued that racially segregated schools were a violation of the Equal Protection Clause.

The final amendment which was passed in the years following the Civil War was the 15th Amendment. The 15th Amendment was ratified and became a part of the Constitution on March 30th, 1870. The 15th Amendment states:

Section 1. *The right of citizens of the United States to vote shall not be denied or abridged by the United States or by any State on account of race, color, or previous condition of servitude.*

Section 2. *The Congress shall have power to enforce this article by appropriate legislation.*

This amendment granted voting rights to the new citizens. Even though former slaves had become citizens with the passage of the 14th Amendment, very few were being allowed to vote across the South. The passage of the 15th Amendment was intended to ensure that all citizens were allowed to vote, regardless of race or color.

However, even after the passage of the 15th Amendment, many African Americans were not allowed to vote. Throughout the late 1800s and first half of the 1900s, many different efforts were made to prevent blacks from voting. Poll taxes, literacy tests, and violence were all means used to suppress minorities and prevent them from participating in elections.

Buffalo Soldiers

During the late 1800s and early 1900s, a group of American soldiers became known as buffalo soldiers. Who were the buffalo soldiers? Why were they known by this name?

On September 21st, 1866, the US 10th Cavalry regiment was formed at Fort Leavenworth, Kansas. It consisted entirely of African Americans who were serving in the United States Cavalry. There had been all-black units during the Civil War, but this was the first of its kind during peacetime. It was these soldiers, as well as the African American regiments of the 9th Cavalry, the 24th Infantry, and the 25th Infantry that became known collectively as the buffalo soldiers.

These soldiers were used extensively during the Indian Wars of the late 1800s. From 1866 through the 1890s, they participated in numerous military campaigns throughout the western half of the United States. In fact, it was their involvement with Native

Buffalo soldiers during the Spanish-American War.

Americans that eventually led to the nickname of "buffalo soldiers".

There is much debate over which tribe first used the "buffalo soldier" nickname. According to different sources, it may have been the Cheyenne, Comanche, or Apache. There is also debate over why the nickname was used. The most common belief is that the title was used out of respect for their bravery and fighting ability. Others have stated that the Native Americans used this term because the soldiers' dark skin and hair reminded them of buffalo.

Aside from their efforts in the Indian Wars, buffalo soldiers served in many other capacities as well. They escorted the US Mail, helped build roads, kept the peace between feuding farmers and ranch owners, and even served as some of the earliest park rangers in national forests.

The buffalo soldiers saw action in other American wars as well. They were involved in the Spanish-American War in 1898 as well as the Philippine-American War from 1899 to 1903. The buffalo soldiers were also a part of the US involvement in the Mexican Revolution in 1910. In 1916, they assisted General John Pershing in the ultimately unsuccessful manhunt for Pancho Villa in Mexico.

The buffalo soldiers became well-known for their fighting abilities and skill as soldiers. Throughout their history, they were complimented by both allies and enemies for their bravery. From 1866 to 1918, twenty-two buffalo soldiers were awarded the Medal of

Honor.

The legacy of the buffalo soldiers has been honored in various ways. There have been numerous songs written about them, including "Buffalo Soldier" written and performed by Bob Marley. There has also been a film, *Buffalo Soldiers*, which was made in 1997 and stars Danny Glover.

<u>*Hiram Revels*</u>

The first African American senator in United States history was Hiram Revels. How did Revels become a senator? How long did he hold this position?

Hiram Rhodes Revels was born in 1827 in Fayetteville, North Carolina. Despite living in the South, his parents were not slaves, but instead were free blacks who were of mixed African and European ancestry. While still a boy, Hiram became an apprentice barber to his older brother who owned a barber shop.

Revels attended Union County Quaker Seminary and Darke County Seminary before becoming an Episcopalian minister. In the 1840s and 50s, he worked as a preacher throughout the Midwest. He ministered in Illinois, Ohio, Tennessee, Missouri, Kansas, and Louisiana. In many of these places, he met with opposition for trying to preach the Bible to African Americans. Once he was even imprisoned for his ministry.

Hiram Revels

During the Civil War, he served as a chaplain in the United States Army. He also assisted in recruiting two black regiments to fight for the Union. Following the war, he renewed his ministry and settled in Natchez, Mississippi. In 1869, Revels was elected to the Mississippi State Senate, representing Adams County.

At the time, United States senators were not elected by popular vote. Instead, they were elected by a vote of the state legislature. Mississippi had been without senators since the Civil War because the previous senators had resigned their positions when Mississippi seceded. In 1870, the Mississippi state senate voted for Hiram Revels to fill one of these two vacancies.

Southern Democrats were highly opposed to Revels taking his seat as a senator. The issue was debated for two days. Democrats argued that Revels was not qualified to be a senator since one of the qualifications was being a citizen of the US for at least nine years. African Americans had not been regarded as citizens until the passage of the 14th Amendment in 1868, therefore, they argued, he had only been a citizen for two years.

Those who supported Revels' appointment argued that he had voted for many years, which qualified him as a citizen. Additionally, they argued that the fundamental reason the Civil War had been fought was to end the subordination of the black race.

On February 25th, 1870, the senate voted in favor of allowing Revels to take his seat. He was sworn in and became the first African American to sit in the United States Senate. As senator, he quietly and diligently fought for the equality of African Americans. During his brief tenure in the US Senate, he impressed reporters with his oratory abilities. His time as senator came to an end on March 3rd, 1871.

After finishing his time in the US Senate, Revels went on to become the president of Alcorn Agricultural and Mechanical College (now known as Alcorn State University) where he also taught philosophy. He also briefly served as Mississippi's secretary of state.

Plessy v. Ferguson (1896)

Plessy v. Ferguson *is one of the most controversial cases in the history of the Supreme Court. Who was Plessy? Why did this case become so important?*

The state of Louisiana passed the Separate Car Act in 1890. This law stated that separate accommodations were required on trains for white passengers and African American passengers.

There were many in Louisiana who thought this law was unfair, including railroad companies who had no desire to purchase additional cars to meet the specifications. Therefore, a group of concerned citizens persuaded Homer Plessy to violate the law so he could be arrested. Their intention was to use Plessy's case to challenge the legality of the Separate Car Act.

In June of 1892, Plessy (who was only 1/8th African American, but still considered black by Louisiana law) boarded a train in New Orleans. He sat down in the "Whites Only" car and was promptly asked to leave by a detective (who had been hired for the specific purpose of arresting Mr. Plessy). When Plessy refused to leave, he was arrested on the charge of violating the Separate Car Act.

When the case (then known as *Homer Adolph Plessy v. The State of Louisiana*) went to court, Plessy claimed that the law violated his 14th Amendment rights to equal protection under the law. However, the presiding judge, John Ferguson, ruled against Plessy and he was ordered to pay a fine of $25.

The case was appealed to the Supreme Court of Louisiana and then again to the U.S. Supreme Court. In April of 1896, the Supreme Court heard oral arguments in the case and eventually reached a 7-1 decision. Their decision stated that the Louisiana law in no way violated the 14th Amendment. Finally defeated, Plessy pled guilty and paid his $25 fine in January of 1897.

Plessy v. Ferguson *ushered in the era of "separate but equal".*

Plessy v. Ferguson was a significant moment in the history of the Supreme Court, as well as the history of the nation. It helped solidify the legal basis for the "separate but equal" doctrine which would become the law of the land throughout the first half of the 20th Century. Segregated facilities for whites and African Americans would become the norm in most large communities. While these segregated facilities were certainly separate, they were rarely equal.

The decision established in *Plessy v. Ferguson* would help shape and define America for decades to come. The "separate but equal" doctrine would not be overturned until 1954 when the Supreme Court heard the case *Brown v. The Board of Education of Topeka, KS.*

Jim Crow Laws

From the 1880s through the 1960s, many American states enforced what came to be known as "Jim Crow" laws. What were Jim Crow laws? Why were they known by this name?

In the years following the Civil War, white southerners went to extensive lengths in an effort to restrict the rights and freedoms of African Americans. Ten of the eleven former Confederate states passed new constitutions, or amended their existing constitutions, in an effort to disenfranchise black voters. For example, in Louisiana, by 1910 there were only 730 African Americans registered to vote. This was significant, considering that African Americans represented a majority of the population in some southern states.

There were many different methods used to prevent blacks from voting. In some instances, they used poll taxes (a fee that had to be paid in order to vote). Since many African Americans were poor, they could not afford to pay the tax, therefore, they were not allowed to vote. Other locations would use literacy tests to prevent African Americans from voting. These were tests to verify whether someone could read or not. Most blacks of this era were under-educated and were not able to read the required text.

In many cases, these literacy tests were manipulated by the test administrator so the test was virtually impossible to pass. For example, the test-taker might be asked to read an extremely complex passage from the Constitution, or asked to read it in a very short amount of time. They might also be asked to explain what they had just read.

These measures prevented many poor and uneducated whites from voting as well. However, many of these laws included what was known as a Grandfather Clause. Such a clause might state that "if your grandfather voted in the 1840 election, then you are exempt from this law". Since only whites were allowed to vote in that election, it was said that these poor, uneducated whites had been "grandfathered in".

With no black voters, or office holders, African American interests went overlooked by state legislatures. In fact, white-controlled state legislatures were able to pass laws that systematically segregated American life and established African Americans as second-class citizens. Every aspect of day-to-day life was becoming segregated, from restaurants and hotels, to railway cars and schools.

In 1896, these segregation laws were legally challenged in the Supreme Court in a case known as *Plessy v. Ferguson*. Homer Plessy was challenging a Louisiana state law which required African American passengers to sit in a separate car on trains. Plessy was arrested for violating this law on June 7, 1892 after he boarded the "whites only" car of the train. The Supreme Court determined that racial segregation was legal, as long as the separate facilities were equal to each other. Thus, with the *Plessy v. Ferguson* decision, "separate but equal" became the law of the land.

All facilities quickly became segregated and remained that way throughout the first half of the 20th Century. For example, there were schools for whites and schools for African Americans. There were "white libraries" and "black libraries". However, the African American facilities were frequently under-funded by state legislatures and lacked proper resources to be effective.

There were few limits to what places could be segregated. African Americans were not allowed in white eating establishments. Public facilities were required to include both white restrooms and black restrooms. Separate parks were also constructed so that white children and African American children did not play together.

Some states went to even more extreme measures. For example, there was an Alabama law which forbade white men and black men from playing billiards together. A Georgia statute outlawed African American barbers from cutting a white woman's hair. There was

*The term "Jim Crow" was taken from a popular
song and dance routine from the 1830s.*

also a Georgia law that stated African American base-ball teams could not play on a field if they were within two blocks of a playground devoted to white children.

These segregation laws became collectively known by the name "Jim Crow" laws. The name was taken from a popular song-and-dance routine performed by Thomas D. Rice in the 1830s. Rice was a white per-former who would dress as a black man and sing a song titled "Jump Jim Crow". Throughout the 1800s, the term "Jim Crow" came to be used to describe Afri-can Americans.

Jim Crow laws were challenged periodically throughout the 1900s, but the most significant blow came in 1954. That year, the Supreme Court heard a case known as *Brown v. the Board of Education of Topeka, KS*. A black family was challenging the notion of segregated schools because their daughter was re-quired to attend a school that was a mile away from her home (there was a white school only seven blocks away). The Supreme Court ruled that segregated schools were unconstitutional. As a result, all school districts across the country were required to integrate (something which did not happen for many more years in some areas).

African Americans and other civil rights supporters continued to work throughout the late 1950s to bring an end to the Jim Crow era. However, segregation continued to be a reality in many facets of life into the 1960s. Finally, on July 2, 1964, the passage of the Civil Rights Act of 1964 outlawed discrimination in public places, including restaurants, hotels, stores, and other workplaces.

Sharecropping

In the years after the Civil War, many African Americans survived by sharecropping. What was sharecropping? How long did it last?

Sharecropping is an agricultural system in which a tenant farmer works the land and raises the crop for a landowner. The farmer and the landowner then split the crop when it is harvested. Sharecropping can be found throughout history in many different cultures, from Ireland and Scotland, to India and Pakistan, and even Africa.

In the United States, sharecropping was first largely seen in the years after the Civil War. After the war ended, all slaves were given their freedom. This left the South with multiple dilemmas. While the former slaves were now free, they had no employment or other means to support themselves and their families. Additionally, plantation owners no longer had the large workforce necessary to raise and harvest their

Sharecroppers in 1941

crops.

Sharecropping became one of the more efficient solutions to this issue. Under the sharecropping system, a landowner would provide a plot of land which the sharecropper would work. The landowner could also provide housing, tools, farming implements, seeds, and even mules if necessary (it is important to remember that each situation was different, so what was or was not being provided may have varied from one sharecropper to another). When the crop was harvested, the sharecropper received a portion of the crop, which he could then sell to provide for his family.

While sharecropping was not ideal, it was seen as a definite improvement over the life of slavery because of the independence and freedom. Sharecroppers typically signed contracts to work for the plantation owner. It was also viewed as a step up from being a mere hired laborer who worked for a wage. In the sharecropping system, the farmer and the plantation owner had a shared interest in the success of that year's crop.

This system also led to a form of credit known as a crop-lien. Under the crop-lien system, a merchant would allow the sharecropper to purchase food and supplies throughout the year on credit. When each year's crop came in, the farmer would then pay off his debt by selling his portion of the crop to the merchant. In this fashion, merchants and plantation owners were able to prevent sharecroppers from ever achieving true financial independence, since they were almost always in debt.

Sharecropping continued to exist throughout the latter half of the 19th Century and the first half of the 20th Century. By the 1930s, there were more than three million African American sharecroppers throughout the nation. However, as farming became more mechanized, there was no longer a need for largescale labor forces to raise and harvest crops. As a result, most sharecroppers moved to cities where they could find jobs in factories.

Booker T. Washington

One of the most prominent African Americans at the beginning of the 20th Century was Booker T. Washington. Why was Washington so well-known? What type of policies did he advocate?

Booker T. Washington was born in 1856. His mother was a slave living in Virginia. His father was an unidentified white man, believed to be a planter who lived nearby. His mother eventually married a freedman, Washington Ferguson, and Booker adopted the last name Washington in honor of his step-father. As a boy, he worked in salt furnaces and coal mines to help his family earn money.

He studied at the Hampton Institute. This was a school specifically designed to educate freedmen. His performance at the Hampton Institute led to the school's president recommending that Washington become the director of the newly-created Tuskegee Institute in Alabama. The Tuskegee Institute was a

Booker T. Washington

"normal school", which meant it was set up to instruct teachers.

The new school opened in 1881, and at first, did not even have its own building. Washington purchased a plot of land and personally oversaw construction of the school's permanent location. The students built the school themselves, making bricks and constructing classrooms and other buildings.

Washington believed that education was the key to African American success. The Tuskegee Institute taught African American teachers basic skills that they could then take to rural communities throughout the South. He felt that learning to read and acquiring either industrial or agricultural skills were the most important things that African Americans could be taught. This knowledge would help them become self-sufficient, productive members of society.

Booker T. Washington gained national prominence in 1895 when he delivered an address in Atlanta. In this speech, he encouraged blacks to be patient and continue working towards full participation in American society. The speech is considered one of the pivotal moments in African American history and launched Washington onto the national stage. However, Washington's views were not shared by all African Americans. Many, including W.E.B. Du Bois, felt that this approach was too soft. However, in the face of this criticism, Washington continued to believe that a confrontational approach would only be disastrous.

As a result of his efforts, Washington developed

good relationships with wealthy men such as John D. Rockefeller, Andrew Carnegie, and many others. These men became financial benefactors to his education efforts. By utilizing private donations from these wealthy men, Washington was able to help build more than 5,000 schools throughout the South.

Washington died in 1915, at the age of 59. The cause of death was attributed to extremely high blood pressure. Since his death, Washington has been honored in many different ways. In 1940, he became the first African American to appear on a postage stamp. He was also the first African American to have his image on a coin, the U.S. half-dollar, in 1946. There are also more than forty public schools across the nation which bear his name.

Booker T. Washington helped countless African Americans achieve a higher level of education. Through reading, writing, and learning industrial skills, many blacks achieved financial success and raised themselves from poverty. Perhaps most importantly though, the learning institutions he established assisted African Americans in understanding the American legal system. This would help pave the way for the Civil Rights Movement of the 1960s.

<u>*George Washington Carver*</u>

Throughout the late 1800s and early 1900s, George Washington Carver became an influential scientist and agricultural expert. What contributions did he make that were significant? How is he remembered today?

George Washington Carver was born as a slave in Diamond Grove, Missouri. The exact date of his birth is not known, but it was most likely in either 1864 or 1865. Slavery was abolished in 1865, but young George and his parents continued living with their former masters, Moses and Susan Carver. The couple helped raise George and his older brother as if they were their own. Susan Carver helped George learn to read and write, and she encouraged his intellectual curiosity.

In 1886, George traveled to Kansas, where he homesteaded a 17 acre farm. He plowed the fields by hand, raising rice, corn, and other types of produce.

By 1890, he was living in Indianola, Iowa, where he started studying music and painting. His art instructor recognized that Carver had a fascination with painting plants and flowers, so she suggested that he study botany.

This encouragement led him to enroll at Iowa State Agricultural College in Ames, Iowa. He was the first African American student enrolled at the university (and would eventually go on to be the first black faculty member at the school as well).

Booker T. Washington, head of the Tuskegee Institute, asked Carver to become the head of Tuskegee's Agricultural Department in 1896. Carver accepted the position, which he held for the next 47 years. There he taught an entire generation of black farmers how to be self-reliant.

Throughout his teaching career, Carver stressed certain values to his students. He taught them to be clean, both inside and out, and to always be considerate to women, children, and the elderly. He also informed his students that they should not look up to the wealthy, nor look down at the poor, and to win with grace, but lose without complaining.

Carver also introduced methods of crop rotation, as well as new varieties of crops which became staples throughout the South. He knew that crop rotation would replenish much needed nutrients in the soil. Peanuts, soybeans, sweet potatoes, and cowpeas were also consumable products that gave Southern farmers alternatives to growing cotton. Because these crops

George Washington Carver

restored nitrogen to the soil, it also helped improve cotton yields.

Carver is best known for the work he did with peanuts. He did many experiments with peanuts and discovered a number of uses for them. In fact, Carver suggested more than 300 uses for peanuts, ranging from axle grease to creating a substitute for buttermilk. Other items he claimed could be made from peanuts included shoe polish, shaving cream, ink, and concrete, amongst many others.

In 1920, Carver spoke at the United Peanut Association of America where he exhibited 145 different peanut-based products. He even testified before Congress in 1922, regarding the importance of the peanut as part of American agriculture. This was a historic moment, for at the time, it was not customary for African Americans to be called to testify as experts in their field. During the last twenty years of his life, Carver became world famous, even meeting with three different American presidents (Theodore Roosevelt, Calvin Coolidge, and Franklin Roosevelt).

George Washington Carver died on January 5, 1943. Even before his death, he was being honored in various ways. A museum opened in 1938, recognizing his work with peanuts, as well as displaying much of his artwork. In 1953, a national monument was opened in his honor. This became the first national monument dedicated to an African American, as well as the first national monument dedicated to someone who was not a president.

Carver's life might be summed up best by the epitaph on his headstone. It reads: *He could have added fortune to fame, but caring for neither, he found happiness and honor in being helpful to the world.*

The NAACP

For more than a hundred years, the NAACP has been fighting for the rights and freedoms of African Americans. How did the NAACP come into being? What years was it most significant?

Following a race-related riot in 1908, it became apparent to many people that a nationwide civil rights organization was needed. In the spring of 1909, W.E.B. DuBois, Ida B. Wells, Archibald Grimke, Mary White Ovington, and six others established an organization that would officially become known as the National Association for the Advancement of Colored People (NAACP). The members of this founding group were diverse, consisting of both African Americans and whites. Some were socially-minded individuals, one was a journalist, and one was even from a former slave-owning family.

The NAACP's mission was "to promote equality and rights and to eradicate caste or race prejudice among the citizens of the United States..."   They also strived to secure the right to vote as well as justice in the courts and education and employment opportunities for African Americans.

Moorfield Storey, a white lawyer from Boston, served as the organization's first president.   The organization grew quickly.   By 1914, there were more than 6,000 members across the nation.   Some early successes included a boycott of the film *Birth of a Nation*, which glorified the Ku Klux Klan, and gaining the right for African Americans to serve as officers in the military during World War I.

Amongst its earliest goals was to overturn the Jim Crow laws which had legalized "separate but equal" facilities.   The group initiated lawsuits with the purpose of challenging these segregation laws.   Several of these court cases were heard by the Supreme Court. The culmination of this effort was *Brown v. the Board of Education of Topeka, KS*.   In this decision, the Supreme Court determined that "separate but equal" schools were unconstitutional.

In the 1950s and '60s, the NAACP was heavily involved in the Civil Rights Movement.   In 1955, they helped organize the bus boycott in Montgomery, Alabama, which successfully resulted in the integration of the Montgomery bus system.   The association played a major role in many other such boycotts, sit-ins, marches, and other demonstrations throughout the late 1950s and early 1960s.

In the mid-1960s, the NAACP began heavily promoting the passage of federal civil rights legislation. These goals were achieved with the passage of the Civil Rights Act of 1964 and the Voting Rights Act of 1965. The NAACP lost much of its influence towards the end of the 1960s. However, it continues to exist today. The organization still promotes the rights of African Americans and fights for equality and justice under the law.

*NAACP leaders posing with an
NAACP recruitment poster.*

The Tulsa Race Riot

One of the worst race riots to ever occur in the United States happened in Tulsa, Oklahoma. What precipitated the riot? What happened in the aftermath?

Between the years of 1910 and 1920, the city of Tulsa was experiencing enormous growth. The population was soaring as people from all over the country made their way to Tulsa to find work in the blossoming oil industry. As Tulsa grew, Greenwood grew as well.

Greenwood was the African American district, just north of Tulsa. By 1921, Greenwood had a population of more than 15,000 and a host of successful businesses including doctors, lawyers, movie theaters, hotels, and restaurants. Its business district was so successful that Greenwood had become known throughout the nation as "The Black Wall Street". Greenwood had become the wealthiest African American community in the nation.

Many poor whites living in Tulsa became jealous of the success Greenwood was experiencing. Young men had returned from fighting in World War I and were unable to find work in Tulsa. This mounting frustration greatly contributed to the events that would occur on May 31st and June 1st of 1921.

On May 30th, 1921, a nineteen-year-old African American shoe shiner, Dick Rowland, entered an elevator in the Drexel Building. The elevator operator was a seventeen-year-old white female named Sarah Page. It is unclear what happened, but experts speculate that Dick Rowland lost his balance and reached out to stabilize himself. Miss Page believed she was being assaulted and screamed, which caused Mr. Rowland to run away in fear. Rowland was apprehended by the police and charged with assault.

This incident was reported by the *Tulsa Tribune* in an exaggerated and sensational fashion. In turn, a group of angry white citizens arrived at the courthouse that evening with the intentions of hanging Dick Rowland. Likewise, a large group of blacks arrived at the courthouse with the purpose of protecting Rowland. Tensions were high between the two groups and a scuffle broke out. During the altercation, shots were fired. Suddenly, the entire city erupted into a sea of violence.

The white mob crossed the railroad tracks into Greenwood and began leveling the community. Fire-bombs were thrown at businesses and homes were burned to the ground, sometimes with families still trapped inside. Many people were shot as they attempted to run away, while others were dragged to death behind vehicles.

Black citizens did not intend to stand idly by while their homes were destroyed and neighbors were killed, so they fought back. Some, who had recently returned from fighting in Europe, began digging trenches and fortifying positions. Greenwood virtually became a warzone.

By the morning of June 1st, Greenwood had been turned into a smoking pile of rubble. The mayor of Tulsa had appealed to the Oklahoma governor to send the National Guard. However, the National Guard did not arrive until late on the morning of June 1st. By this time, most of the fighting had died down. Black rioters were rounded up by the thousands and taken to detention centers.

The official death toll from the riot was 39. However, many bodies were hidden or disposed of before they could be counted. Historians estimate that the actual number of dead could be as high as 300. More than 800 were wounded. Thirty-five city blocks were destroyed by fire. This included 191 businesses, a junior high, several churches, and a hospital. More than 10,000 Greenwood residents were left homeless.

Dick Rowland was never charged with a crime. Sarah Page dropped the charges against him, and Rowland was escorted from Tulsa shortly after the riot and never returned to the city.

Following the Tulsa Race Riot, there was a concentrated effort to omit the incident from state and local history. Newspaper articles about the riot were destroyed and it was rarely mentioned in state history textbooks. Many residents of the state grew up without knowing the violence had ever occurred. Finally, in 1996, the state created a commission to study the riot and create a historical account so that the memory of the events could be preserved.

The city of Greenwood never recovered completely. It took more than ten years to rebuild the area. Today, this region is known as North Tulsa.

This image shows Greenwood on fire during the Tulsa Race Riot of 1921.

The Great Migration

In the 1910s and 20s, a large number of African Americans moved from the South to other parts of the country. Why did they move? What kind of impact did this have on the nation?

In 1900, most African Americans in the United States lived in Southern states. In fact, 90% of the African American population still lived in the South. However, many began to move into Northern and Midwestern states, such as Michigan, Illinois, Pennsylvania, and New York.

The reasons they were moving varied from family to family. In some cases, they were hoping to find jobs in steel mills, automobile factories, meatpacking plants, or working for the railroad. Some were searching for better schools and educational opportunities. Others were hoping to escape the racism and violence that African Americans were experiencing in the South.

Most who left the South were heading for larger Northern cities. Chicago, New York City, Detroit, Philadelphia, Pittsburg, and Cleveland all experienced significant surges in population. For example, in 1910, the African American population of Detroit was approximately 6,000. By 1930, this number had increased to 120,000. Nationwide, only an estimated 740,000 African Americans lived outside of the South in 1900. As the 20th Century progressed, this number eventually rose to more than 10 million living in other regions of the country.

The Great Migration was one of the largest and fastest movements ever by a group of people who were moving from one part of a nation to another. This is especially true when considering that the movement was not caused by some kind of immediate threat or danger. This migration had many different ramifications for the nation.

This painting is titled "During World War I, there was a great migration north".

As black populations rose, many Northern cities became increasingly more integrated. African Americans were working alongside recent European immigrants as well as other white residents. These cities also became important centers for African American culture. Newspapers, churches, businesses, and political organizations were all established by African Americans as part of a movement to redefine black culture. Harlem (a neighborhood in New York City) became the center of much of this activity. Musicians, artists, and writers flocked to the area, bringing about the era that eventually became known as the Harlem Renaissance.

There were also some negative impacts of the Great Migration. Many African Americans who moved north did experience racism in their new cities. In some neighborhoods, white residents moved away, having no desire to live with black neighbors. This resulted in some places, such as Harlem, having an almost exclusively black population.

Obviously, another significant impact of the Great Migration was the changing demographics of the South. Every Southern state experienced a loss in African American population, especially in the rural regions. African Americans made up more than 50% of the populations in both Mississippi and South Carolina. Texas, Louisiana, Alabama, and Georgia had populations that were more than 40% black. Within just a few decades, these numbers would be reduced to less than 30% in nearly every one of those states.

The Harlem Renaissance

Throughout the 1920s, Harlem experienced a cultural and intellectual explosion that became known as the Harlem Renaissance. Who was involved in the Harlem Renaissance? What was its ultimate impact?

Harlem is a neighborhood in New York City which has a very large African American community. Harlem became a destination for African Americans throughout the early 1900s as part of the Great Migration. As more blacks made Harlem their home, it increasingly became well-known as an African American cultural center. Poets, writers, artists, musicians, and philosophers were all key parts of the movement.

One of the key components of the Harlem Renaissance was music. Jazz performers including Jelly Roll Morton, Fats Waller, Duke Ellington, and Louis Armstrong perfected their music, which became very popular amongst white audiences. It was also during this era when the piano was incorporated into the jazz style

Fats Waller was one of the early jazz musicians that was responsible for what came to be known as the Harlem Renaissance.

of music. Traditionally, jazz bands had included primarily brass instruments.

Intellectuals such as W.E.B. Du Bois and Marcus Garvey argued and debated issues of racism, ethnic pride, and other topics related to African American life. Poets such as Langston Hughes introduced a new form of poetry known as jazz poetry. African American literature of the era included themes such as how slavery had impacted the African American culture and how to combat stereotypes of black Americans.

African American clothing also drastically changed during the Harlem Renaissance. Black men started wearing zoot suits. These were suits which featured long coats with padded shoulders and wide lapels. Women wore low-slung dresses, silk stockings, and open-toed slippers. Both genders wore hats with wide brims. Leopard skin items also became popular, as they were seen as a connection to traditional African garb.

The Harlem Renaissance had a profound impact on the United States, as well as the world. African American artists, musicians, and writers began to be respected on an international level. Not only were white audiences listening to and enjoying black music, but white composers and musicians began incorporating African American rhythms and harmonies into their own pieces. The Harlem Renaissance also helped to change the world's perception of African Americans. Prior to the 1920s, blacks were thought of as uneducated farmers. However, thanks to the Harlem Re-

naissance, a new image of sophisticated and intellectual African Americans began to emerge.

<u>*Langston Hughes*</u>

Langston Hughes was one of America's greatest poets. Where was Langston Hughes from? How is he remembered today?

Langston Hughes was born on February 1, 1902 in Joplin, Missouri. He came from an interracial family, in which two of his great-grandfathers were white. Hughes spent most of his early life living in Lawrence, Kansas with his grandmother. As an adolescent, he also spent time in Illinois and Ohio.

As a young adult, Langston worked many different jobs, from being a crewman on board a ship, to a busboy, and the personal assistant to a historian. He also attended Lincoln University, an African American college in Pennsylvania. After earning a degree from Lincoln, he established a residence in Harlem (in New York City), where he would live for the remainder of his life.

His first published poem was "The Negro Speaks of

Rivers", which was published in 1921. This became his most famous and well-known work of poetry. He would eventually go on to write more than fifteen books of poetry throughout his life. Hughes strived to portray the life of the average African American through his poetry. He attempted to tell the story of working-class and poor blacks in America. He also sought to challenge racial stereotypes and speak out against social conditions of the day.

Hughes was not just a poet, as he became a prolific author as well. He wrote several different novels and collections of short stories. His bibliography also includes several non-fiction books, including two autobiographies. Additionally, Hughes wrote twelve plays and eight works for children.

Langston Hughes died at the age of 65 on May 22, 1967 from complications following abdominal surgery. His ashes are interred in Harlem, beneath the floor of a building named in his honor.

Hughes is remembered today as one of the most important figures of the Harlem Renaissance. This was a period during the 1920s in which Harlem became the center of a rebirth of African American culture, including poetry, literature, art, and music. However, the impact of Hughes' life went far beyond Harlem. His influence was felt throughout the nation, not only in the world of literature, but in jazz music, politics, and the overall culture of the African American community.

His memory is honored in a number of different

Langston Hughes

ways. City College in New York City annually awards the Langston Hughes Medal to an influential African American writer. There have been several schools named in his honor, his home in Harlem is regarded as a historical landmark, and in 2002, Hughes was recognized as part of a series of postage stamps honoring Black Heritage.

W.E.B. Du Bois

W.E.B. Du Bois was one of the most influential African American thinkers of the 20th Century. What topics did Du Bois care about? What was his overall influence on the African American culture?

William Edward Burghardt Du Bois was born in Great Barrington, Massachusetts on February 23, 1868. As a young man, he decided to attend Fisk College in Nashville, Tennessee. He was able to attend through generous donations from his local church, as well as support from neighbors. It was during college that he experienced segregation enforced by law for the first time. After earning a bachelor's degree from Fisk, he enrolled at Harvard. He worked his way through three years of attending Harvard, paying for school with loans from friends, scholarships, and summer jobs. He earned a second bachelor's degree in 1891, and in 1895, Du Bois became the first African American to

William Edward Burghardt Du Bois

receive a PhD from Harvard University.

Early in his career, he taught at Wilberforce University, the University of Pennsylvania, and Atlanta University. He published his first important study in 1899; it was titled "The Philadelphia Negro". This was considered a breakthrough accomplishment because it was the first scientific sociological study done in the United States.

As the new century began, Du Bois became involved in the Pan-African Movement. This was a movement which encouraged solidarity for Africans around the world. He became an influential part of the first Pan-African Conference in London and drafted a letter to the world. In this letter, he encouraged nations to fight against racism and grant political rights to those of African ancestry. He also encouraged self-governance of the European colonies in Africa.

Du Bois became a well-known critic of Booker T. Washington. Washington believed that African Americans should accept segregation in exchange for vocational training and other basic educational opportunities. Du Bois adamantly disagreed with this position, arguing that blacks should fight for equal rights. Through his writings and published papers, Du Bois popularized the term "the talented tenth". This referred to the one-tenth of African Americans that would eventually become leaders of the race, a position they could only achieve by continuing their education, writing books, and becoming involved in social change.

Du Bois became an influential and successful writer. His most important work was *The Souls of Black Folk* which has been praised as being nearly as important to the African American community as *Uncle Tom's Cabin*.

Du Bois helped co-found the National Association for the Advancement of Colored People (NAACP). His primary task with the NAACP was to edit the organization's monthly publication, *The Crisis*. Du Bois wrote many articles for *The Crisis*, and it became incredibly popular under his guidance. The publication had a readership of 100,000 by the year 1920.

Throughout the 1920s, Du Bois clashed with Marcus Garvey, a leading intellectual who was originally from Jamaica. Garvey preached a message of "Africa for Africans" and believed that African Americans should work towards complete separation rather than attempting to integrate. Du Bois disagreed with this strategy and referred to Garvey as reckless and fraudulent.

Du Bois was initially a supporter of the Harlem Renaissance. He actively promoted the creative efforts of African American artists. He even published an article in *The Crisis* titled "A Negro Art Renaissance". However, as the 1920s progressed, he became discouraged that not enough artists and musicians were using their talents to promote the African American cause.

Du Bois continued to fight for African American rights throughout the remainder of his life. He died on August 27, 1963 at the age of 95 while living in Ghana,

Africa. Today, he is remembered as one of the most influential African American philosophers of the 20th Century. His birth home in Massachusetts is registered as a historical landmark, and his life and career has been honored in many different ways.

Marcus Garvey & James Weldon Johnson

Two of the most prominent intellectuals associated with the Harlem Renaissance were Marcus Garvey and James Weldon Johnson. What did these men do? How did they advance the Harlem Renaissance?

Marcus Garvey was born in Jamaica in 1887. Early in his life he became a passionate supporter of the Pan-African Movement. This was a philosophy which promoted the solidarity of Africans throughout the world. While still living in Jamaica, he founded the Universal Negro Improvement Association (UNIA) which boasted more than 65,000 members.

In 1916, he moved to Harlem, where he began publicly speaking about his causes. He became convinced that people of African descent should return to their homeland in Africa, and as a result, he attempted to revitalize the nation of Liberia, a country which had been founded by the American Colonization Society in the late 1800s. He hoped to build railroads, factories,

Marcus Garvey

and colleges in the country. He even established the Black Star Line, a shipping company that was to transport goods and even people to Africa. However, after pressure from foreign nations who hoped to colonize Liberia, he eventually abandoned the plan.

While Garvey gained a considerable following in the United States and worldwide, not everyone was a fan. Other black leaders of the day, such as W.E.B. Du Bois, criticized Garvey and claimed he was a dangerous enemy to African Americans.

In 1925, Garvey was accused and convicted on charges of mail fraud. Garvey and his supporters claimed the charges had more to do with his outspoken political views than any wrongdoing. He was sentenced to the Atlanta Federal Penitentiary and eventually deported back to Jamaica. Although he remained active for many more years, Garvey's "Back to Africa" movement lost most of its momentum in the latter half of the 1920s.

James Weldon Johnson became politically active in the 1910s. In 1916, he started working for the National Association for the Advancement of Colored People (NAACP). Johnson organized parades and other mass demonstrations, protesting lynching throughout the South and race riots in the North.

Johnson was selected as the Executive Secretary of the NAACP in 1920. This meant that he was essentially its chief operating officer, a position which he held for ten years. During that time, he fought valiantly against the crime of lynching. In 1921, his efforts led to the House of Representatives passing the Dyer Anti-Lynching Bill. However, this bill was defeated in the Senate on more than one occasion and never became law.

Throughout the 1920s, he also encouraged the movement that eventually became known as the Harlem Renaissance. He helped promote young African American authors and worked to assist them in becoming published. He also became well-known for his own poems, novels, and songs.

James Weldon Johnson

Louis Armstrong

One of the greatest trumpet players who has ever lived was Louis Armstrong. How did Armstrong become so well-known? How is he remembered today?

On August 1, 1901, Louis Armstrong was born into a very poor family. He and his mother lived in a dangerous, poverty-stricken neighborhood of New Orleans known as "the Battlefield". He dropped out of school when he was only eleven years old and started singing in the streets for money. However, he was also a troublemaker. He ended up in the New Orleans Home for Colored Waifs, a home for juvenile delinquents. While there, he learned to play the cornet, a brass instrument similar to the trumpet.

Armstrong was released from the boys' home when he was fourteen and eventually went to work, hauling coal during the day and performing music at night. Throughout the late 1910s and early 1920s, Armstrong continued to master the trumpet, the instrument he

Louis Armstrong

would eventually become famous for playing.

In 1922, Armstrong joined Joe "King" Oliver's Creole Jazz Band in Chicago. The Creole Jazz Band became one of the most popular bands in Chicago, which was the heart of jazz music in the early 1920s. The star of the band was the standout young trumpet player nicknamed Satchmo (short for satchel mouth).

Eventually, Armstrong branched out on his own. He progressively became more and more famous throughout the decade. He became well-known for his groundbreaking approach to trumpet playing, as well as introducing the nation to new techniques such as scat singing. Scat is a vocal technique in which sounds are improvised. While Armstrong did not invent scat singing, his performances are amongst the earliest and best-known examples.

Satchmo became legendary not only for his talent on the trumpet, but for his unique vocal qualities as well. He had a distinct, low-pitch gravelly voice that was instantly recognizable. His most well-known songs include "What a Wonderful World", "When the Saints Go Marchin' In", and "We Have All the Time in the World".

Armstrong died in his sleep in July of 1971. His funeral was attended by many other performers who mourned the loss of such an amazingly talented man with a wonderful personality. Bing Crosby, Frank Sinatra, Dizzy Gillespie, Ella Fitzgerald, Count Basie, Ed Sullivan, and Johnny Carson were all honorary pallbearers.

Today, Louis Armstrong is thought to be one of the most influential jazz performers of all time. He has also inspired performers in other genres of music. Bing Crosby once referred to Armstrong as "the beginning and end of music in America."

Duke Ellington

One of the most legendary jazz musicians and bandleaders to emerge from the 1920s was Duke Ellington. Why did Duke Ellington become so famous? How is he remembered today?

Duke Ellington was born on April 29, 1899 with the given name of Edward Kennedy Ellington. His friends called him "Duke" because his suave manner and sophisticated style of dressing reminded them of nobility. As a boy, his mother enrolled him in piano lessons, although he was more interested in playing baseball at the time.

As he became a teenager, he started taking his musical training more seriously. He wrote his first piece of music, "Soda Fountain Rag" at the age of fifteen. He started observing and mimicking other talented piano players and continued to learn more about reading music and writing musical compositions.

Ellington made a decision as a young man that

Duke Ellington

would change his life forever. He left his home in Washington DC and moved to Harlem in New York City. There, he would become a part of what would eventually be known as the Harlem Renaissance. This was a period of time in which many talented African American entertainers, writers, and artists were performing and working in the Harlem area.

Throughout the 1920s, Ellington continued to perfect his craft, and he gained a reputation for his talent and abilities. In 1927, he was offered a unique opportunity. He and his eleven-piece band became the house band at the famous Cotton Club. Wealthy white audiences flocked into the club each night to hear Ellington and his band perform. The stage shows featured not only Ellington's music (much of which he wrote himself), but also included dance numbers, comedy, and other types of entertainment.

Most importantly though, the Cotton Club had a weekly radio broadcast. Ellington was heard by audiences across the nation. This allowed his music to be appreciated by not only the high-priced clientele of the Cotton Club, but the average person as well. Ellington charmed audiences both in person and on the air with his wit and elegant style.

As the 1920s progressed into the 1930s, Ellington and his band only became more and more popular. He remained one of the most popular figures in music for years, producing classics such as "I Got it Bad", "Mood Indigo", and of course, "It Don't Mean a Thing (If It Ain't Got That Swing)."

Ellington earned an impressive twelve Grammy Awards and has received numerous other honors. In 2002, he was named one of the 100 Greatest African Americans, and in 2009, his image was placed on a quarter representing the District of Columbia.

The Cotton Club

In the late 1920s, the Cotton Club became one of the most legendary establishments in American history. What was the Cotton Club? How did it become so famous?

The Cotton Club got its start in 1920, when heavyweight boxing champion Jack Johnson opened a supper club in Harlem. Three years later, the club was sold to notorious bootlegger Owney Madden. Madden used the club as a way to distribute high-priced alcohol to a ritzy upper-class crowd.

As the 1920s progressed, the Cotton Club became well-known as one of the most popular, and exclusive, nightclubs in the country. It was a "whites-only" establishment, and wealthy customers would line up to enjoy the club's mixture of entertainment and alcohol.

The club catered to the legendary and the famous. On any given night, it would not be surprising to see Jimmy Durante, George Gershwin, or Al Jolson making a visit. Mae West and Irving Berlin were also known to frequent the club.

Despite the club's white clientele, the performers at the venue were all African American. Some of the finest singers, dancers, actors, comedians, and instrumentalists that Harlem had to offer all performed at the Cotton Club. The Cotton Club musical revues, known as *The Cotton Club Parade*, became legendary.

Many talented entertainers got their start, and their first taste of fame, in the Cotton Club. Fats Waller, Louis Armstrong, Count Basie, Lena Horne, Billie Holliday, Bill "Bojangles" Robinson, and Sammy Davis Jr. all performed at the Cotton Club. However, throughout the late 1920s, the true star of the club was the leader of the house band, Duke Ellington. Each week, a live radio broadcast aired from the Cotton Club, and Ellington became known nationwide as a composer, piano player, and band leader.

The patrons of the Cotton Club were high-paying, wealthy customers. When they entered the club, they expected to see the best that Harlem had to offer. As a result, many of the Cotton Club performers were well-paid, especially when compared to other African Americans living in Harlem. However, they were strictly forbidden from mixing with or associating with the guests. They were not allowed to drink or linger in the club. The entertainers performed twice a night, at midnight and again at 2:00 AM. After each performance, they would relax in the basement of a neighboring building.

The Cotton Club continued to be popular into the 1930s. In 1936, the club moved to a new location outside of Harlem. Additional branches of the Cotton Club also existed in Chicago and California. The Cotton Club closed its doors forever in 1940 after allegations of tax evasion and the changing tastes of the public simply passed it by.

Billie Holliday was amongst the many performers who got their start performing at the Cotton Club.

Jesse Owens

Jesse Owens is one of America's greatest Olympic heroes. What sport did he participate in? Why was it such a memorable Olympics?

When Jesse Owens was in junior high, he discovered his love for running. In fact, it was the encouragement of his junior high track coach which set him off on the right foot in life. In high school, he gained a lot of attention by tying the world record in the 100 yard dash. He also won the high school national championship in the long jump.

He attended Ohio State University, where he continued to gain notoriety. In 1935, he won four NCAA championships in individual track events, and in 1936, he won four more. These eight individual championships is a record which still stands today. However, possibly his most incredible feat in college occurred at a track meet in 1935. He set world records for the long jump, the 220 yard sprint, and the 220 yard hurdles.

He also tied the world record for the 100 yard dash—and he did all four in less than an hour.

In 1936, the Summer Olympics was held in Berlin, Germany. This was an important Olympics because Germany was controlled by Adolph Hitler and the Nazis at that time. Hitler had convinced the German people that they were mentally and physically superior to the rest of the world—and all other races were inferior. He hoped to prove this at the 1936 Olympics.

Jesse Owens proved otherwise though. Owens went to the 1936 Olympics and put on a show. He was awarded three individual gold medals, winning the 100 meter sprint, the long jump, and the 200 meter sprint. He also secured a fourth gold medal by participating on the 4x100 meter relay team.

Hitler, who was supposed to congratulate each champion after their victory, left the Olympic Stadium without acknowledging Owens' accomplishments.
Owens returned to the United States a hero, but his life after the Olympics was not an easy one. The US was still very much segregated, and Owens was denied many opportunities. He ran a dry cleaning business, filed for bankruptcy, was prosecuted for tax evasion, and at one point was even reduced to racing against horses to try and earn money.

Finally, in the late 1960s, the US government named him as a Goodwill Ambassador. He traveled around the world to speak to different governments and businesses, promoting sportsmanship and American ideals everywhere he went.

Jesse Owens

Jesse Owens died in 1980 after a battle with lung cancer, and his life has been honored in various ways since his death. The United States Post Office has issued two different stamps featuring his likeness, each year the nation's top track & field athlete is given the Jesse Owens Award, and in 1990 he was given the Congressional Gold Medal. He is also still remembered as one of the most legendary Olympic heroes the world has ever known.

Joe Louis

One of the greatest heavyweight boxing champions in the history of the sport was Joe Louis. Why was Joe Louis so well known? How long was he the champ?

Joe Louis was born in rural Alabama in 1914, but his family moved to Detroit in 1926 (as part of the "Great Migration"). It was in Detroit where young Joe grew to love the sport of boxing. He started training at a local youth recreation center where he lost his very first fight. In no time at all, though, he racked up numerous victories and won the recreation center championship.

As Louis matured as a boxer, he started attracting interest from professional boxing promoters. Around 1935, he began fighting in the professional ranks and gained national attention when he knocked out former heavyweight champion Primo Carnera in six rounds. When he defeated another former heavyweight cham-

Joe Louis

pion Max Baer, Joe became one of the prime contenders for the heavyweight title.

Louis was all set to battle James Braddock for the heavyweight championship when he fought Max Schmeling for the first time. Schmeling was a German fighter who was not meant to be a serious challenge to Louis, but Schmeling took the bout seriously, studying Louis's fighting style intently. On June 19, 1936, Schmeling defeated Louis in 12 rounds, handing him the first loss of his professional career.

Louis did go on to knockout Braddock in 1937, claiming the heavyweight championship. However, he said he would not truly feel like the champ until he defeated Schmeling.

The rematch, dubbed "The Fight of the Century", was set for June of 1938, and it would go on to become one of the most legendary sporting events ever. Schmeling had become a German national hero and was held up by Adolph Hitler as a shining example of how Germans were physically superior to all others. Meanwhile, everyone in the Depression-plagued U.S. was supporting Louis, marking the first time an African American had become a nationwide hero.

Over 70,000 people filled Yankee Stadium to watch the fight live, while an estimated 70 million more around the world listened on the radio, making it the largest audience ever to listen to a radio broadcast. The fight lasted only two minutes and four seconds. Joe Louis attacked Schmeling with a barrage of punches, knocking him down three times, while

Schmeling was only able to land two blows. After Schmeling was knocked down the third time the fight was stopped, and Louis was declared the victor.

Joe Louis went on to be the heavyweight champion for twelve years (from 1937 to 1949). He defended his title successfully 25 times, a record which still stands today. In 1982, he was given the Congressional Gold Medal for his outstanding achievements. Still to this day, Joe Louis is remembered as one of the greatest heavyweight boxers of all time.

<u>Jackie Robinson</u>

Jackie Robinson is remembered as one of the most legendary baseball players to ever play the game, but what did he do to become so famous?

In 1919, Jackie Robinson was born in Georgia, the youngest of five children in a family of sharecroppers (they farmed and paid a portion of their crop as rent). From an early age, he excelled at many different sports, including football, baseball, basketball, and track & field. In high school, he even played tennis!

While attending UCLA, he continued to prove his athleticism by becoming the first student in school history to letter in four sports: football, basketball, baseball, and track & field. His best sport was easily football, and he had plans of playing professionally as a running back. However, his pro sports dreams were sidetracked by World War II. He was drafted in 1942, serving his country in a segregated cavalry unit where he was selected for Officer Candidate School.

Jackie Robinson

After the war, a friend encouraged Robinson to try out for the Kansas City Monarchs, one of the franchises in the Negro American League (an African American baseball league). Even though baseball was arguably his worst sport, he signed a contract in 1945 to play for $400 a month (that would be over $5,000 a month today!).

After one successful season with the Monarchs, he garnered interest from more than one major league franchise. Even though Major League Baseball was segregated at the time (whites only), there were several teams considering the idea of integrating. Finally, in late 1945, the general manager and president of the Brooklyn Dodgers, Branch Rickey, decided that Jackie Robinson might just be the African American player to break this barrier. He signed Robinson to a contract, and Jackie was sent to the minor leagues for the 1946 season.

As the 1947 season began, it was apparent that Robinson was ready for big league baseball. Yet the question remained, was Major League Baseball ready for him. He made his debut with the Brooklyn Dodgers on April 15, 1947 (playing 1st base rather than 2nd, which became his standard position throughout his career).

His first season was not easy as many people did not want Major League Baseball to become integrated. He was spit on and heckled by fans (in some cases, even fans of his own team). Players from opposing squads hurled racial epithets and insults at him as he rounded the bases. He was subject to rough, overly-physical contact with players intentionally colliding with or sliding into him. The St. Louis Cardinals even threatened to go on strike (refusing to play) if Robinson took the field against them.

Robinson managed to maintain his composure and endure this torment. Instead of lashing out against his critics, he let his abilities on the field speak for him. That first season, he batted .297, hit 12 homeruns, and led the league with 29 stolen bases. He was also selected as the "Rookie of the Year".

As his career progressed, he proved to be an incredibly gifted athlete, and because of his success, he was joined by other outstanding African American players. Because of his efforts at integrating Major League Baseball, he is recognized today in various ways. His number, 42, has been permanently retired by all of Major League Baseball, and there are numerous awards, buildings, and even stadiums named in his honor. Baseball's Rookie of the Year award is now known as the "Jackie Robinson Award", and, of course, he is in the Baseball Hall of Fame.

Tuskegee Airmen

During World War II, the Tuskegee Airmen became some of the most well-known pilots of the era. Why were the Tuskegee Airmen significant? Why were they known by this name?

Prior to World War II, no African Americans were allowed to serve as pilots in the US military. Many had desired to serve in this capacity during World War I, but were rejected by the Army on the basis of their race. However, in April of 1939, Congress designated funds for the training of African American pilots.

Many questioned whether there were enough African Americans wanting to fly to make this effort worth it. According to numbers taken in the 1940 census, there were only 124 African American pilots in the entire nation. However, as the program to train pilots began, there was an over-abundance of volunteers, and the War Department only accepted the most intelligent and physically able candidates.

African American pilots during World War II

The flight training program for African American pilots was established at Tuskegee University. Tuskegee University was an African American university which already had an existing pilot training program for civilians. The military's flight training program officially began in June of 1941, and only one year later, there were more than 3,000 individuals stationed at Tuskegee. This number included the pilots-in-training, as well as those working to help train them.

The first group ready for combat was the 99th Pursuit Squadron (later known as the 99th Fighter Squadron) which shipped out on April 2nd, 1943. They flew their first mission over the volcanic island of Pantelleria in the Mediterranean Sea on June 2nd, 1943. At one point during the war, the 99th gained attention for setting a record of destroying five enemy aircraft in less than four minutes.

In early 1944, the 332nd Fighter Group was sent overseas as well, which consisted of three all-black fighter squadrons. The 332nd flew missions over Czechoslovakia, Austria, Hungary, Poland, and Germany. Additionally, they also completed missions over Sicily, Anzio, Normandy, and the Rhineland. The 332nd earned the nickname "Red Tails" because the tail section of each plane was painted a distinctive red.

Aside from the 99th Fighter Squadron and the 332nd Fighter Group, a bomber group was trained as well. The 477th Bombardment Group was trained at Tuskegee to fly B-25s. However, the war came to a conclusion before their training was complete.

Tuskegee eventually trained 992 pilots in between 1941 and 1946. Tuskegee pilots flew 1,578 combat missions and 179 bomber escort missions. They destroyed 262 enemy aircraft and more than 950 enemy vehicles (including railroad cars, trucks, tanks, and other vehicles). Eighty-four of these pilots lost their lives and another 32 became prisoners of war. Ninety-six Tuskegee pilots were awarded the Distinguished Flying Cross. Three Tuskegee airmen went on to become generals.

The Tuskegee Airmen have been remembered in many different ways. For example, there have been many books written regarding their exploits. The airfield at which they trained is now the Tuskegee Airmen National Historic Site. In 2007, the Tuskegee airmen were collectively given the Congressional Gold Medal. There have also been two major motion pictures, *The Tuskegee Airmen* (1995) and *Red Tails* (2012).

De Jure vs. De Facto Segregation

Segregation has long been an issue in the United States of America, as well as other countries. Segregation can generally be broken into two different types. What are those two types? How does one differentiate between the two?

The two different forms of segregation are de jure segregation and de facto segregation. De jure is a Latin phrase which means "according to law". This means that de jure segregation is legally established and enforced by law. De facto is a Latin phrase which means "in fact" or "in reality". Therefore, de facto segregation is not enforced by law, it merely exists based on where people choose (or are financially able) to live, work, and go to school.

De jure segregation became law in the United States in the 1890s. More and more states began passing segregation laws with the intention of keeping African Americans separated from whites, thus forcing them into the role of "second-class citizens". These segregation laws were challenged by the Supreme Court case of *Plessy v. Ferguson* in 1896. However, the Supreme Court ruled that these laws were constitutional, as long as the segregated facilities were "separate but equal". Therefore, de jure segregation became the law of the land. These "separate but equal" laws became collectively known as the Jim Crow laws and remained in place throughout the first half of the 20th Century.

In 1954, another Supreme Court case, *Brown v. the Board of Education of Topeka, KS*, was the first step in removing de jure segregation from the United States. The Supreme Court determined that separate but equal schools were unconstitutional. Other aspects of life continued to be segregated by law throughout the 1950s, '60s, and even into the 1970s in some places. However, through the diligent efforts of civil rights activists, de jure segregation is no longer legal in the United States.

De facto segregation was not enforced by law, but could be just as effective at segregating different groups of people. In the first half of the 20th Century, African Americans left the South in droves and moved to larger cities in the North. At the time, many white residents in these communities had no desire to live near African Americans, so they moved out of the cities and into suburbs. This had the effect of leaving large inner-city urban areas with almost exclusively black populations and suburbs, on the outskirts of cities, with almost exclusively white populations. This evacuation of the inner-cities for the suburbs has become known as "white flight".

Other measures were unofficially practiced to ensure that these communities remained segregated. In some cases, banks would refuse loans to black customers if they intended to purchase a home in a known white area. Some neighborhoods would over-inflate the price of their homes in order to discourage prospective black buyers. Some homeowners even made secret agreements with their neighbors that they would not sell their home to African Americans.

Many of these types of practices are still in use today in places around the country. As a result, de facto segregation remains a part of American society. However, most would agree that the United States has come a long way since the days of the Jim Crow era.

This sign shows an example of "de jure" segregation.

Brown v. Board of Education (1954)

At some point in their school careers, almost every American student is taught about Brown v. Board of Education, but who was Brown? What was this famous court case about?

In the first half of the 20th Century, throughout the United States, segregation was the law of the land. Schools, as well as other public institutions and businesses, were commonly segregated on the basis of race. This had been upheld in the Supreme Court case *Plessy v. Ferguson.*

Linda Brown was an African American third grader who attended Monroe Elementary School in Topeka, KS. This was the all-black school she was required to attend because of the segregation laws in place at the time. To reach her school each morning, she had to walk six blocks to reach the bus stop before traveling by bus another mile to reach her destination. Meanwhile, Sumner Elementary School (an all-white school) was only seven blocks from her home, but she was not allowed to attend it because she was African American.

Her father, Oliver Brown, attempted to enroll her in Sumner Elementary. After he was refused, he took his case to court. He was actually one of several parents who filed a class-action suit against the School Board of Topeka, KS. Even though there were thirteen parents involved in the case, it will be Mr. Brown's name that history will always remember.

A district court initially ruled in favor of the school board, but the case was appealed to the United States Supreme Court. The parents' case was argued by Thurgood Marshall, who later went on to become a Supreme Court justice. The case was heard in front of the Court for the first time in the spring of 1953. The justices were unable to reach a decision and asked to hear the case again in the fall.

Brown v. the Board *paved the way for integrated schools across the United States.*

The Court's final ruling was unanimous. By a 9-0 vote, the justices determined that state laws which created separate schools for African Americans were unconstitutional, stating that these laws violated the Equal Protection Clause of the 14th Amendment. Newly appointed Chief Justice Earl Warren wrote the Court's opinion over the case.

This was a landmark Supreme Court decision and major victory for the Civil Rights Movement. Even though this decision set the stage for integration to take place, it would be many years before it was seen in reality. Topeka Schools began integrating as early as 1953, but would not see full integration until 1956.

This issue was actually addressed by the Court in 1955. Many school districts had asked for lenience in the desegregation process. The Court revisited its previous decision, which became known as *Brown v. the Board II*, and stated that desegregation should occur "with all deliberate speed" (meaning 'as fast as possible'). Supporters of desegregation did not like this phrase, because they felt it gave communities an opportunity to resist and delay the desegregation process.

This fear was well-grounded, as some communities avoided integration for years. In Virginia, there was a movement to close schools rather than see them integrated. Texas, Arkansas, Alabama, and several other states also resisted the integration process throughout the 1950s and even into the 1960s! However, integration was eventually achieved, and today, children are allowed to attend the school nearest to their home, thanks to the decision reached in *Brown v. Board of Education.*

Thurgood Marshall

One of the most legendary African Americans of the 20th Century was Thurgood Marshall. Why did Marshall become so prominent? What contributions did he make to society?

Thurgood Marshall was born on July 2, 1908, in Baltimore, Maryland. His father was a railroad worker, while his grandfather and great-grandfather had both been slaves. His mother was a teacher, and she taught him from an early age about the importance of the United States Constitution.

He studied at Lincoln University, where at first he did not take his classes seriously. However, he eventually became involved with the debate team and also started becoming interested in political and social issues. He attended law school at Howard University, graduating first in his class in 1933. While at Howard, he became deeply interested in the topics of segregation and discrimination.

Thurgood Marshall

Upon graduating, Marshall started his own private law practice. He also began working closely with the National Association for the Advancement of Colored People (NAACP). He became a member of the NAACP's national staff in 1936, and by 1940, he was the Executive Director of the NAACP Legal and Educational Defense Fund.

He fought tirelessly against segregation, arguing many cases in front of the Supreme Court. Marshall eventually argued thirty-two cases in front of the Court, winning twenty-nine of them. The most famous of these was *Brown v. the Board of Education of Topeka, KS (1954)*. In this case, Marshall successfully argued that laws establishing different schools for black and white children were unconstitutional. The Supreme Court agreed, and this began the process of school integration throughout the United States.

In 1961, President John Kennedy appointed Thurgood Marshall as a judge to the United States Court of Appeals, Second District. He held this position for four years, when in 1965, President Lyndon Johnson appointed Marshall to the position of United States Solicitor General. He was the first African American to hold this position.

A vacancy on the Supreme Court opened in 1967, after the retirement of associate justice Tom C. Clark. President Johnson called on Marshall again, this time asking him to fill this vacancy. Marshall's appointment was confirmed by the US Senate on August, 30, 1967, making him the first African American Supreme

Court Justice.

Marshall maintained his position on the Supreme Court for 24 years, displaying strong support for the US Constitution and individual rights. He retired from the Court in 1991 and was replaced by Clarence Thomas, who is also African American.

Thurgood Marshall died from heart failure in 1993. He has been memorialized in many different ways since his passing. The Federal Judiciary Building in Washington D.C. is named in his honor, as well as many other buildings throughout the United States, including an international airport in his hometown of Baltimore.

The Little Rock Nine

On May 17, 1954, the Supreme Court issued its decision in Brown v. the Board of Education of Topeka, KS. This decision stated that racially segregated schools were unconstitutional. Following this decision, many school districts across the nation faced the difficult challenge of integrating. One of the worst incidents involving integration occurred at Little Rock Central High School. What happened there? How was the situation resolved?

In 1955, the Little Rock school board approved a plan for the gradual integration of Little Rock's public schools. The plan would be implemented in the fall of 1957. It was decided that only one high school would be integrated that year. Other schools would follow in subsequent years.

Nine African American students were selected to attend the previously all-white Little Rock Central High School. These individuals were selected because they were excellent students with good attendance records.

Those opposed to integration threatened to protest and claimed they would physically barricade the school, refusing entry to the black students. The governor of Arkansas, Orville Faubus, even deployed the Arkansas National Guard on September 4, 1957 in support of the segregationists. The entire nation became interested in the situation as television and newspapers showed a line of soldiers blocking these nine students from entering the school.

The "Little Rock Nine" being escorted into Little Rock Central High School by National Guardsmen.

The mayor of Little Rock made a plea to President Dwight Eisenhower, asking him to send federal troops to assist in the integration process. On September 24th, the president ordered the 101st Airborne Division of the US Army to Little Rock. He also federalized the entire Arkansas National Guard. This meant that the National Guard, who just days before had prevented the African American students from entering the school, were now ordered to protect them from the segregationist protesters.

As the nine students entered the school, agitators shouted out insults and spat at them. Inside the building, things were not much better. The students were subjected to verbal and physical abuse throughout the school year, and the white students who perpetrated these incidents were rarely punished. One of the African American students even had acid thrown in her eyes.

Governor Faubus refused to be defeated, though. As the 1957-58 school year came to an end, Faubus began making plans to bring a halt to the integration process. That summer, he argued that continued integration would lead to an increase in violence. In early September of 1958, he signed legislation which closed all Little Rock public schools. The schools remained closed the entire year. This led to resentment of African Americans in Little Rock because many whites saw them as the cause of the closed schools.

Schools re-opened in the fall of 1959, and integration continued as planned. Black school children still received much physical and verbal abuse from their white classmates, but as time progressed, school eventually proceeded as usual.

The Little Rock Nine have not been forgotten. There have been many books written about their plight and their stressful first year attending Little Rock Central High School. There have also been multiple movies made chronicling this experience. There is also a memorial dedicated to them on the grounds of the capital building in Little Rock. In 1999, the group was awarded the Congressional Gold Medal. This is the highest award which can be given to a civilian by Congress.

<u>The University of Alabama Integration</u>

In June of 1963, Governor George Wallace attempted to prevent two African Americans from enrolling at the University of Alabama. Who were these students? How did Governor Wallace attempt to do this?

In 1954, the Supreme Court reached its decision in *Brown v. The Board of Education of Topeka, KS*. This decision stated that "separate but equal" schools for different races were unconstitutional. At that point, all public schools nationwide, including colleges, were required to integrate.

As of 1963, the University of Alabama had yet to enroll any black students. Hundreds of qualified African Americans had applied, but the university refused every application for admission, using the most insignificant of reasons to disqualify each candidate. Two students, Vivian Malone and James Hood, applied for entry to the University of Alabama in 1963. They were exceptional students and their applications were in good order. A federal district judge ordered that the students be admitted to the university.

Governor George Wallace threatened that if the African American students attempted to enroll, he would stand in front of the door and refuse to allow them entry. On June 11th, Malone and Hood arrived, and Wallace followed through with his threat. He personally barricaded the door, refusing to allow them inside.

At this point, Vivian Malone was escorted to her dormitory, where she was told to wait until the situation could be resolved. She was instructed that she could eat in the cafeteria by herself, if she desired. To her surprise, when she ate her meal she was joined by several white students.

After Governor Wallace refused to step aside, Deputy Attorney General Nicholas Katzenbach sought the help of President John Kennedy. President Kennedy federalized the Alabama National Guard and ordered them to assist in the integration process.

Later that afternoon, a second attempt was made to enroll the students. With the assistance of the National Guard, Katzenbach asked Governor Wallace to step aside, which he did. Malone and Hood entered the building and successfully enrolled. As they entered, they were greeted with applause from those within the building who supported integration.

Vivian Malone went on to become the first African American graduate of the University of Alabama. The events surrounding her and James Hood's enrollment have been depicted in film on more than one occasion. A prominent scene in the 1994 film *Forrest Gump* features the famous incident, as does the 1997 film *Wallace*.

Governor George Wallace carrying out his symbolic threat to stand in front of the entrance at the University of Alabama.

James Meredith & the Integration of the University of Mississippi

James Meredith became the first African American to attend the University of Mississippi. What events occurred that allowed this to happen? Did Meredith do anything significant after attending college?

James Meredith was born in Kosciusko, Mississippi in 1933. After graduating from high school, he enlisted in the United States Air Force. In 1961, he applied to the University of Mississippi. At the time, the school was still only admitting white students, even though the US Supreme Court had determined that segregated schools were unconstitutional. He was denied for admission, so he applied again. His application was denied the second time as well.

With the assistance of the NAACP Legal Defense and Educational Fund, Meredith filed a lawsuit on May 31st, 1961. His claim was that the only reason he had been rejected by the University of Mississippi was

James Meredith

his race. He had been a good student in school and also had an excellent record in his military service.

The case was heard by both the US District Court for the Southern District of Mississippi and the US Court of Appeals for the Fifth Circuit. It was ruled that Meredith had the right to attend the University of Mississippi. This decision was appealed to the US Supreme Court, but the Court supported the decision of the Appeals Court.

The governor of Mississippi, Ross Barnett, announced that no Mississippi school would be integrated while he was governor. The Mississippi state legislature also attempted to prevent Meredith's enrollment by passing a law which stated that someone's college admission could be denied if that person had committed a crime of "moral turpitude". This law was directly aimed at James Meredith, since the only blemish on his record had been an arrest for "false voter registration".

Throughout the month of September in 1962, Governor Barnett continued to prevent the integration from occurring, even though the university was ready to accept Meredith as a student. After several phone calls with US Attorney General Robert Kennedy, Barnett agreed to allow the integration to take place.

On September 29th, a riot ensued on campus as National Guardsmen and federal troops clashed violently with white protesters who opposed the integration process. There was considerable damage to university property, several cars were burned, and two men even lost their lives. With 500 US Marshals accompanying him, Meredith arrived on campus and enrolled on October 1st. This is considered one of the landmark events in the history of the Civil Rights Movement.

Life on campus was not easy for Meredith after he enrolled. He was the target of frequent harassment from other students. However, he endured through the final two semesters of his school career, and in 1963 he became the first African American to graduate from the University of Mississippi.

In 1966, Meredith led the March Against Fear. This was a 220 mile march from Memphis, Tennessee to Jackson, Mississippi, which began on June 6th, 1966. Meredith hoped to help blacks in Mississippi overcome their fear of violence as well as encouraging them to register to vote. During the second day of the march, Meredith was shot and wounded. Others vowed to continue the march in his name, and before long, more than 15,000 marchers were participating. It became the largest Civil Rights march in Mississippi state history, and more than 4,000 African Americans registered to vote during the event. Before the march ended, Meredith was able to recover from his wounds and join his fellow demonstrators as they arrived in Jackson.

The Montgomery Bus Boycott

In December of 1955, the African American community in Montgomery, Alabama began a boycott of all city buses. Why did they start the boycott? Was it successful?

In 1900, the City of Montgomery passed a law which segregated passengers on the basis of race. Buses had a "whites only" section at the front and a "black" section near the rear of every vehicle.

However, the number of rows was not fixed. It had become standard practice that, as more white passengers boarded the bus, the African American passengers were required to give up their seats and move further back. Another section of this law stated that black passengers were not even allowed to sit on the same *row* as a white passenger!

Very few people challenged the law, until one day in 1955. On December 1st, 1955, 42-year-old Rosa Parks paid her fare, boarded a bus, and took an appropriate

Rosa Parks sitting in her seat on the bus

seat at the front of the "black" section. As the bus continued on its route, more passengers boarded. When the "whites only" section reached capacity, the driver asked Parks and three others to give up their seats. Mrs. Parks refused and was arrested for her defiance.

Martin Luther King Jr. and other leaders of the Civil Rights Movement decided to use her arrest as a means to challenge the unjust law. They implemented a citywide bus boycott, and African Americans refused to ride on the buses if the segregation laws remained in place.

To compensate, black citizens organized carpools, and African American taxi drivers lowered their fare to 10 cents (the same as bus fare). Others walked, rode bicycles, or even horses and mules to reach their destinations. Churches across the country took up collections to donate slightly-worn shoes to the people of Montgomery, some of which were walking as much as 20 miles at a time!

In retaliation, whites who supported segregation laws resorted to violence. Boycotters were physically attacked, and the homes of Dr. King and others were firebombed. King and 89 others were eventually arrested for their role in the Montgomery Bus Boycott. King was fined $500 for conspiring to interfere with a local business and was also required to spend two weeks in jail.

In the end, none of the resistance mattered. Over 75% of bus passengers were African American, therefore, the city buses lost a significant amount of business as the protest continued. Finally, on December 20th, 1956, after 381 days, the boycott came to an end as the City of Montgomery integrated all buses.

While this was an important victory in the fight against segregation, the Montgomery Bus Boycott had a larger impact. It jump-started the Civil Rights Movement and helped thrust Martin Luther King Jr. to the forefront of that movement.

Rosa Parks

Rosa Parks is one of the most iconic figures of the Civil Rights Movement. Who was Rosa Parks, and what did she do to become so famous?

Rosa Parks was born in Tuskegee, Alabama in 1913. She grew up and lived in Alabama, where she held various jobs from housekeeper, to hospital aide, and seamstress. In December of 1955, she was working at a department store, when her life took an unexpected turn.

On December 1st, 1955, at about 6:00 PM, Mrs. Parks was just getting off work when she boarded a bus in Montgomery, Alabama. The buses were segregated, and she selected a seat on the front row of the "black" section. As the bus continued to pick up passengers, the "whites only" section filled up.

The understood custom, although it was not officially a law, said that as the white section filled up, the black customers were expected to continue moving

Rosa Parks with Martin Luther King Jr.
in the background.

back. When the bus driver asked her to give up her seat to a white passenger, she refused.

The bus driver informed her that if she did not relinquish her seat, he would be forced to call the police. She still refused. The driver then had her arrested. She was charged with disorderly conduct and fined $10, plus $4 in court costs.

Her arrest sparked the beginning of the Montgomery Bus Boycott. This was a 381 day boycott of the Montgomery Bus system, which successfully brought an end to the practice of segregating passengers on city buses.

Following her arrest, Mrs. Parks became a notable figure in the Civil Rights Movement. However, her life was not without its difficulties. Because of her stance on segregation, she lost her job at the department store where she had been working, and her husband was forced to quit his job as well.

Over the years, she held several different jobs, from seamstress, to hostess, and finally secretary to a US Representative (a position she held until she retired in 1988). She quietly lived out the remainder of her life in Detroit, where she died in 2005 at the age of 92.

Rosa Parks left a lasting legacy. She has had everything from streets, to highways, schools, parks, libraries, and even a train station named in her honor. She also has a statue in the U.S. Capitol's National Statuary Hall (a chamber in the U.S. Capitol Building that is devoted to sculptures of prominent Americans).

More importantly, the events surrounding her arrest on that December day in 1955 ignited the modern Civil Rights Movement, bringing important leaders such as Martin Luther King Jr. to the head of that struggle.

Rosa Parks mugshot on the day of her arrest

The Freedom Riders

One of the monumental efforts during the Civil Rights Movement was known as the Freedom Rides. Who were the Freedom Riders? What were they trying to do?

In 1961, a group of well-meaning college students (mostly from Northeastern states) and other activists made the decision to challenge Southern segregation laws. Their plan was to make a bus trip across the South, from Washington DC to New Orleans. The group was made up of blacks and whites who were going to ride the bus in an integrated fashion (rather than segregated seating, as was the custom in Southern states).

Their purpose was to illustrate that these segregation laws were in violation of national law, established by multiple Supreme Court cases, and bring national attention to the fact that segregation was being enforced by use of violence in Southern states.

The first Freedom Ride began on May 4th, 1961. At first, they encountered few problems in states like Virginia and North Carolina. However, as the interracial group moved further into the Deep South, they began to face tough resistance.

In Birmingham, Alabama, Police Commissioner Bull Conner coordinated efforts with the local Ku Klux Klan chapter, with the intention of bringing the Freedom Ride to an end.

On May 14th, Klansmen attacked the first bus (of two). They blocked its path, refusing to allow it to leave the bus station and then slashed the tires. As the bus was forced to stop, a firebomb was thrown into the vehicle. As the bus began to burn, the attackers held the door shut, hoping to burn the Freedom Riders inside.

As the riders managed to escape, they were physically beaten by those who had attacked them. Eventually, highway patrolmen arrived to chase off the violent mob, and they almost certainly prevented the deaths of several Freedom Riders. The passengers were taken to the local hospital, where many were refused treatment.

An hour after the first Freedom Riders were assaulted, the second bus arrived. It was attacked multiple times by two different groups of Klansmen. The passengers were beaten with baseball bats, pipes, and chains.

Despite the violence, the Freedom Riders hoped to continue their mission. They faced violence several more times throughout their journey, and fresh Freedom Riders replaced the wounded as the ride continued. They eventually made it as far as Jackson, Mississippi.

Even though they did not continue all the way to New Orleans, they accomplished their goal in bringing much needed national attention to the issue of segregation in the South. Other rides would follow, and throughout the early 1960s, more than 450 people participated in a Freedom Ride.

Two Freedom Riders trying to clean themselves up after being attacked during their journey

<u>*Emmett Till & Medgar Evers*</u>

One of the key events that triggered the Civil Rights Movement was the murder of Emmett Till. What events led to Emmett's murder? How was Medgar Evers involved in the investigation?

Emmett Till was a fourteen-year-old from Chicago. He had traveled to Money, Mississippi in August of 1955 to visit relatives. It was a Sunday morning when Till and some other boys entered Bryant's Grocery and Meat Market to buy candy. While in the store, Till had an encounter with Carolyn Bryant, the twenty-one-year-old wife of the store's owner, Roy Bryant.

It is unclear what happened between Till and Bryant. By most accounts, Till was thought to have flirted with Carolyn in some way. Bryant was upset by the incident and left the store to retrieve a pistol from her vehicle. After seeing this, the boys decided to leave the area immediately.

On August 28th, 1955, in between 2:00 AM and

3:30 AM, Roy Bryant and J.W. Milam arrived at the home Mose Wright, where Till was staying. They took Till from the home at gunpoint and drove him to a barn where they beat him severely. They put him in the back of a pickup truck and took him to several different locations, beating him more than once. Finally, they tied a 70 pound metal fan around Till's neck with barbed wire and threw him into the Tallahatchie River.

Three days later, his body was found by two boys who were fishing. Till's head had been badly damaged, and he had been shot above the right ear. One eye had been dislodged from its socket, and there was evidence that other regions of his body had been beaten as well. Roy Bryant and J.W. Milam were placed on trial for murder. The trial lasted five days, and despite eye witnesses who identified both men, they were acquitted of the charges against them. The all-white jury only deliberated for 67 minutes.

Emmett Till

Till's murder and the subsequent trial became a national news story and brought race relations in Mississippi to the forefront of the nation's conscience. Till's story became symbolic of the injustices that African Americans were regularly facing throughout the South. Till's death became one of the ultimate sparks that led to the modern Civil Rights Movement in the United States.

As the investigation of Emmett Till's murder unfolded, the NAACP became fearful that the local sheriff's office would not make every effort to find Till's murderers. As a result, the NAACP chose to launch its own investigation into the matter. Medgar Evers, Ruby Hurley, and Amzie Moore were chosen for this task. The trio tracked down potential witnesses and convinced several of them to come forward about what they saw. They also made certain that these witnesses were protected before the trial and saw that they found safety out of town, after the trial had concluded.

Medgar Evers' involvement in the Till investigation, as well as his other Civil Rights activities, made him one of the leading figures in the Civil Rights Movement. As a result, he became the frequent target of white supremacist attacks. In May of 1963, a bomb was thrown into the carport of his home, and in June of that same year, he was nearly run down by a car as he was leaving an NAACP office.

On June 12, 1963, Evers was shot in the back after exiting his vehicle. He was taken to a hospital where he died less than an hour later. Evers, a veteran of the

US Army, was buried in Arlington National Cemetery, where he received full military honors. More than 3,000 people attended his funeral, and his death was mourned across the nation.

Byron De La Beckwith was arrested for the murder on June 21st, 1963. He was placed on trial, but was not convicted of Evers' murder. In 1994, new evidence led to a new trial, and Beckwith was finally convicted for his crime, at the age of 74.

In 2013, Alcorn State University, Medgar Evers' alma mater, erected a statue in his honor to commemorate the 50th anniversary of his death. Special guests from around the world came to honor his legacy.

This statue of Medgar Evers stands on the campus of the University of Mississippi.

Martin Luther King Jr.

Martin Luther King Jr. is remembered for his work in the Civil Rights Movement. How did he get his start? What contributions did he make to the movement?

Martin Luther King Jr. was born in January of 1929. From an early age, Martin showed outstanding intelligence, work ethic, and determination. He skipped two grades in high school and entered college at the age of fifteen. In 1948, he graduated with a degree in Sociology. Along the way, he met and married Coretta Scott, whom he eventually had four children with.

He became a Baptist minister in 1954 at a church in Montgomery, Alabama. It was there in Montgomery where King's career as a civil rights leader began. In December of 1955, an African American woman named Rosa Parks was arrested for refusing to give up her seat on a bus to a white passenger. In protest of this arrest, King and several others helped to implement a city-wide bus boycott.

The Montgomery Bus Boycott brought an end to racial segregation on all Montgomery public buses. The boycott also brought attention to the plight of African Americans and helped thrust Martin Luther King Jr. to the forefront of the Civil Rights Movement.

In 1957, King and several others founded the Southern Christian Leadership Conference. This was an organization made up of black ministers who were committed to advancing civil rights through the use of non-violent protests.

The concept of non-violent protests was essential to King's efforts. He had been heavily influenced by Mahatma Gandhi's non-violent protests against British rule and policies in India, which were extremely successful. Even in the most severe situations, King remained steadfast to the principle of pacifism.

He believed the key to gaining sympathy for the African American cause rested in people seeing the suffering of Southern blacks at the hands of violent segregationists. He felt any physical retaliation would cause people to turn away from their struggle.

One of King's successes using non-violent protest came in 1963 when he organized an effort to challenge the segregation laws of Birmingham, Alabama. The SCLC orchestrated marches and sit-ins in public places, openly violating the "Jim Crow" laws.

King was arrested during the protests, and it was during this stint in jail that he wrote "Letter from Bir

Martin Luther King Jr.

mingham Jail". In the letter he compared the struggle of African Americans to the struggle of those who fought the American Revolution… "We know through painful experience that freedom is never voluntarily given by the oppressor; it must be demanded by the oppressed." In the end, the event was successful, and the "Whites Only" signs came down in many places.

Later in 1963, Martin Luther King Jr. and the Southern Christian Leadership Conference (SCLC) planned a massive event in Washington DC that became known as the March on Washington. The march took place in August of that year and was intended to bring national attention to the plight of African Americans in the South.

More than 250,000 people attended the event, which took place on the National Mall. The highlight of this event was a speech delivered by Dr. King, which today is known as the "I Have a Dream" speech. It is widely regarded as one of the finest speeches ever delivered.

As a result, the Civil Rights Movement came to the forefront of American politics. The U.S. Congress responded by passing the Civil Rights Act of 1964, which outlawed discrimination based on racial or ethnic background.

In 1965, as part of an effort to register African Americans to vote in Alabama, King organized a march from the town of Selma to the city of Montgomery. This effort was met with violent resistance from the police and a mob of angry citizens. The violence against the marchers was so extreme that the day became known as Bloody Sunday (March 7th, 1965). News coverage of the police brutality was broadcast across the nation, and Americans were outraged by what they saw.

Later that month, on March 25th, 1965, the protesters made another attempt to conduct the same march. This time, under the protection of federal authorities, the marchers were allowed to continue into Montgomery unharmed. As a result of the confrontation, Congress passed the Voting Rights Act of 1965, which prohibited states from denying anyone the right to vote on the basis of race or ethnicity.

Dr. King's non-violent resistance to segregation led to many positive changes during the 1960s. However, in 1968, his life came to a tragic and abrupt ending. In March of that year, King went to Memphis, Tennessee to assist with a labor dispute. Sanitation workers were on strike in an effort to gain better pay and improved working conditions.

On April 4th, 1968, at 6:01 PM, King was shot as he stood on the second floor balcony of the Lorraine Motel. He was immediately taken to a hospital, where he was pronounced dead at 7:05 PM. The assassin had been a 40-year-old man named James Earl Ray, who was captured two months later.

King's death prompted riots in Washington DC, Chicago, and many other American cities. However, just days after his death, Congress passed the Civil Rights Act of 1968, which provided equal housing opportunities for all Americans, regardless of race or ethnicity.

Martin Luther King Jr.'s legacy has lived on. Not only did his work bring about the passage of three major pieces of legislation, but his efforts ushered in an era of racial equality which is growing stronger every day. In 1983, President Ronald Reagan signed a bill creating a federal holiday in honor of Dr. King. The holiday is known as Martin Luther King Jr. Day, and it is honored in January, close to the time of his birth.

Letter from Birmingham Jail

On April 16, 1963, Dr. Martin Luther King Jr. wrote a famous letter from Birmingham Jail. But why did he write this letter? And what did it say?

In the early 1960s, Birmingham, Alabama was one of the most heavily segregated cities in America. Blacks and whites were separated in virtually every area of life, and this segregation was strictly enforced by law. In the spring of 1963, Dr. King was in Birmingham, helping to coordinate a non-violent protest movement. The protests were intended to bring an end to the segregation of the city's downtown merchants.

King, along with other civil rights leaders and supporters, organized several different forms of protests including boycotts, marches, and sit-ins at restaurants, libraries, and churches.

Throughout this process, the protests were met with harsh resistance from the police and spectators.

Demonstrators were sprayed with fire hoses, attacked by police dogs, and spat upon by angry bystanders. On April 12th, 1963, Dr. King, along with 50 others, was arrested and taken to Birmingham City Jail.

On that same day, a group of eight white Alabama ministers had published a letter titled "A Call to Unity". In this letter, they suggested that the Civil Rights Movement should be fought in the courts, rather than the streets, and asked that African Americans be patient.

During his stint in jail, Dr. King penned a response to these clergymen. It is this response that has become known as "Letter from Birmingham Jail."
In his response, he stated:

"We have waited for more than 340 years for our constitutional and God given rights... Perhaps it is easy for those who have never felt the stinging darts of segregation to say, 'Wait.' But when you have seen vicious mobs lynch your mothers and fathers at will and drown your sisters and brothers at whim; when you have seen hate filled policemen curse, kick, and even kill your black brothers and sisters... then you will understand why we find it difficult to wait."

Throughout the letter, he spoke eloquently about the plight of African Americans in the U.S., saying that *"We know through painful experience that freedom is never voluntarily given by the oppressor; it must be demanded by the oppressed."* At a later point in the letter, he adds, *"Oppressed people cannot remain oppressed forever. The yearning for freedom eventually manifests itself..."*

The letter was published for the first time in June of 1963. Today, it has been reprinted countless times and is used in high school and college classrooms throughout the country as an example of the mindset and determination that Dr. King possessed.

Martin Luther King Jr. addressing reporters

The March on Washington

On August 28ᵗʰ, 1963, one of the most well-known protest events in United States' history took place in Washington DC. Why is this event so famous? And what were they protesting?

The event that has become known as the March on Washington was officially known as the March on Washington for Jobs and Freedom. It was organized by the Southern Christian Leadership Conference (SCLC), the Congress of Racial Equality (CORE), the Student Non-Violent Coordinating Committee (SNCC), the NAACP, and other leading Civil Rights groups.

Their purpose was to bring the issues of racial inequality and injustice to the forefront of the American political scene.

On August 28ᵗʰ, 1963, thousands of buses, trains, planes, and cars flooded into the nation's capital. The spectacle was held on the National Mall, with the

Thousands gather on the mall in Washington DC for the "March on Washington" which featured Martin Luther King Jr.'s famous "I Have a Dream" speech.

speakers stationed in front of the Lincoln Memorial.
An estimated 250,000 people turned out for the event,
which featured fiery speeches from civil rights leaders
and songs from popular entertainers such as Bob Dyl-
an and Joan Baez.

Television and radio outlets sent more than five
hundred members of the media to give the march the
attention it deserved. The national news exposure the
proceedings received helped to propel the topic of civil
rights into the American consciousness.

While there were more than ten speakers at the
March on Washington, no one's speech was more
highly anticipated than the leader of the SCLC, Dr.
Martin Luther King Jr. King delivered a speech that is
remembered as the "I Have a Dream" speech. In the
speech, he stated:

*I have a dream that one day this nation will rise
up and live out the true meaning of its creed: "We
hold these truths to be self-evident: that all men are
created equal."... I have a dream that my four little
children will one day live in a nation where they will
not be judged by the color of their skin but by the con-
tent of their character... I have a dream that one day,
down in Alabama...little black boys and black girls
will be able to join hands with little white boys and
white girls as sisters and brothers.*

He then concluded his speech with:

*...when we allow freedom to ring, when we let it ring
from every village and every hamlet, from every state
and every city, we will be able to speed up that day*

when all of God's children, black men and white men, Jews and Gentiles, Protestants and Catholics, will be able to join hands and sing in the words of the old Negro spiritual, "Free at last! free at last! thank God Almighty, we are free at last!"

Dr. King's speech at the March on Washington is regarded as one of the finest examples of oratory ever delivered and was voted the greatest American speech of the 20th Century.

The Southern Christian Leadership Conference

One of the most influential organizations during the Civil Rights Movement was the Southern Christian Leadership Conference. How did this organization come into existence? And who started it?

In December of 1956, the Montgomery Bus Boycott came to a successful conclusion. On the heels of that victory, Dr. Martin Luther King Jr. and other prominent civil rights leaders called together more than 60 African American ministers in January of 1957. These ministers jointly created a new organization, which they named the Southern Christian Leadership Conference (SCLC).

The SCLC's goal was to end all forms of racial discrimination and segregation. They sought to achieve this goal by use of non-violent protests, which included boycotts, sit-ins, marches, and other demonstrations.

Martin Luther King Jr. speaking with other leaders of the Southern Christian Leadership Conference

Despite their well-meaning goals, the group initially had great difficulty finding supporters in the African American community. Many African Americans feared that if they participated in demonstrations and protests, it might result in retribution from the white community. They were threatened by the possibility of being fired, or even violence being used against them for such actions.

The SCLC was criticized in many different ways. Some felt the organization was too extreme. This opinion was voiced by those who believed the battle for civil rights should be fought in the court rooms, rather than through direct actions such as protesting. Others criticized the SCLC for not being extreme enough! They felt that *violent* action should be taken against those who supported segregation.

The organization did experience many triumphs, though. In 1963, they orchestrated the "Birmingham Campaign" which successfully brought an end to segregation amongst Birmingham's downtown merchants. They were also at the forefront of organizing the March on Washington in August of that same year.

The group was also instrumental during the Voters' Rights Campaign in Alabama in 1965. This included the dramatic march from Selma to Montgomery and culminated with the passage of the Voting Rights Act of 1965.

Aside from their protest efforts, the SCLC also managed a Citizenship School program. This was intended to teach adult African Americans how to read and write so they could fill out driver's license applications, open bank accounts, and, most importantly, pass voter registration literacy tests.

While its most prominent days were in the 1960s, the SCLC is still alive today. They continue to work, fighting social injustices around the world.

The Civil Rights Act of 1964

The Civil Rights Act of 1964 is one of the most historic pieces of legislation to be enacted. What did this monumental law do? And what circumstances led to its creation?

In May of 1963, Martin Luther King Jr. and the Southern Christian Leadership Conference (SCLC) concluded a successful campaign against segregation in Birmingham, Alabama.

In June of that same year, President John Kennedy delivered a speech in which he asked for a major piece of civil rights legislation. He stated that all Americans should have the right to be served in hotels, restaurants, theaters, and retail stores.

In August, Dr. King and the SCLC, along with five other major civil rights organizations, organized and carried out an event in Washington DC which became known as the March on Washington. This march caused the Civil Rights Movement to become the leading issue on the American political scene.

As a result of the publicity these three events received, politicians in Washington DC were forced to take a serious look at civil rights issues.

President Kennedy continued working to get his civil rights legislation passed for the next several months. However, in November of 1963, he was assassinated in Dallas, Texas. The new President, Lyndon B. Johnson, urged Congress to pass Kennedy's civil rights bill, arguing that nothing could honor President Kennedy's memory more than passing the bill he had fought so hard for.

*President Lyndon Johnson signing the
Civil Rights Act of 1964 into law.*

The bill was presented to the Senate on March 30, 1964. A group of 19 Southern senators attempted to filibuster the bill and prevent its passage. The most ardent opposition came from Senators Strom Thurmond (D-SC) and Robert Byrd (D- WV). Thurmond claimed that the legislation was unnecessary and unconstitutional, while Robert Byrd delivered a speech which lasted 14 hours and 13 minutes!

After filibustering for 54 days, the opposing senators finally relinquished. On June 19th, the U.S. Senate approved the bill, which was finally, and officially, approved by both houses of the U.S. Congress on July 2nd, 1964.

The Civil Rights Act of 1964 outlawed major forms of discrimination against racial, ethnic, national, and religious minorities, and women. It also brought an end to the unequal use of voter registration requirements (meaning that the same requirements had to be applied to all voter applicants). Additionally, it intended to bring about an end to racial segregation in schools, the workplace, and any public facility.

Freedom Summer

One of the most remembered events of the Civil Rights Movement was known as Freedom Summer. What was the purpose of Freedom Summer? How successful was it?

Throughout the first half of the 1900s, very few African Americans could vote in the South. For example, in 1962, only 6.7% of the African American population was registered to vote in Mississippi. In the early 1960s, various efforts were being made by civil rights organizations to get as many blacks registered as possible.

In 1964, a group of students led by the Student Non-Violent Coordinating Committee (SNCC) began planning for what would eventually be known as Freedom Summer. Their goal was to not only register African Americans to vote in Mississippi, but also to start the process of integration and build a network of leadership throughout the African American community.

SNCC recruited on college campuses across the nation and interviewed large numbers of potential volunteers.   Eventually, over 1,000 out-of-state volunteers participated and worked alongside African Americans from Mississippi. Most of the volunteers were white college students from Northern states.

Aside from the volunteer workers, there were also countless others who helped make Freedom Summer possible. Doctors, nurses, and medical students provided emergency care for the volunteer workers and other activists who needed medical treatment. Lawyers also provided free legal services to those who had been arrested for demonstrating.

Some of Mississippi's white residents resented the presence of outsiders who they saw as trying to forcibly change their way of life. There were many acts of violence against the civil rights workers conducted by groups such as the Ku Klux Klan, as well as by local police and sheriff's departments. Throughout the ten weeks of Freedom Summer, more than 1,000 people were arrested, 80 civil rights workers were beaten, 37 churches were bombed, and 30 black homes and businesses were destroyed.

The most notable incident of violence against the Freedom Summer workers was the deaths of James Chaney, Andrew Goodman, and Michael Schwerner, which occurred on June 21st, 1964. Chaney was African American, while Goodman and Schwerner were white. They had been arrested by the Neshoba County deputy sheriff, who was also a Ku Klux Klan member.

After the three boys were released from jail, they were followed and ambushed by Klansmen. Goodman and Schwerner were shot at close range. Chaney was beaten and then shot three times. Their bodies were buried in a nearby earthen dam.

The FBI began investigating the incident, and the entire nation was captivated by the search for the missing boys. FBI agents and members of the military searched through swamps and forests for days. In the process of their investigation, they unearthed eight other bodies of missing African Americans.

Freedom Summer workers James Chaney (top), Andrew Goodman (center), and Michael Schwerner (bottom) were killed by Klansmen on June 21st, 1964.

Eventually, the bodies of the workers were discovered and the FBI arrested 19 suspects. Seven of these were convicted, but none served more than six years in prison for the crime. This represented the first time in the state of Mississippi that whites had ever been convicted for civil rights violations against African Americans. The events surrounding these murders have been loosely depicted in the 1988 film *Mississippi Burning*.

Freedom Summer did not succeed in registering large numbers of African Americans to vote. However, it did have its significance. Prior to the Freedom Summer project, the national media had largely ignored the persecution of black voters and the dangers experienced by civil rights workers in the South. Due to the deaths of Chaney, Goodman, and Schwerner, the entire nation began to pay attention to what was going on in Mississippi and the Deep South.

SNCC

One of the most influential organizations during the Civil Rights Movement was SNCC. What type of events did SNCC organize? What were the group's accomplishments?

In 1960, the Southern Christian Leadership Conference granted $800 to fund a conference which was attended by 126 students from 12 different colleges. The end result of this conference was the creation of the Student Non-Violent Coordinating Committee (SNCC, which is traditionally pronounced as "snick").

SNCC began mobilizing communities across the South, organizing various types of demonstrations to express their displeasure with continued segregation. Their most common method of protest was the sit-in. Protesters would choose a segregated "whites only" restaurant and enter the establishment. They would take seats at the counter, or even on the floor, and refuse to leave.

SNCC would also stage sit-ins at public libraries, public parks, and public swimming pools. At the time, African Americans paid taxes to fund all of these facilities, yet they were not being allowed to use any of them. In many cases, rather than allowing these locations to be integrated, white city leaders would opt for closing the facilities altogether.

In the early 1960s, SNCC members became well-known as the frontline participants in the Civil Rights Movement. SNCC members participated in the Freedom Rides. These were racially-integrated groups that traveled on buses into the Deep South, protesting the South's refusal to integrate.

In 1964, SNCC organized Freedom Summer, an effort in the state of Mississippi to register as many African Americans to vote as possible. The group also organized Freedom Schools, schools that were established in Mississippi as an alternative to the public schools that focused on encouraging social, political, and economic change, as well as developing leadership skills. Over 40 of these schools were eventually opened, and more than 2,500 students attended.

In the mid-1960s, SNCC distanced itself from the mainstream Civil Rights Movement and became more radical in nature. The group shifted from a stance of non-violence and became more militant, adopting the "black power" philosophy. This was a belief that African Americans could come together as a political force and end segregation by whatever means necessary.

"Black power" was popularized by Stokely Carmichael, a Civil Rights activist who became SNCC's chairman in 1966. Under Carmichael's leadership, SNCC continued to become more radical. In December of 1966, the organization ousted all of its white members. Carmichael also began advocating the use of violence to overthrow their white oppressors.

By 1967, SNCC found itself in extreme financial difficulties. Many supporters refused to financially back the organization with its new radical views. It continued to exist throughout the 1960s, but lost most of its earlier influence as many of its top leaders moved on to other organizations. By 1970, SNCC had nearly disappeared; however, some local chapters remained active well into the mid-1970s.

The SNCC logo featured a black hand clasping a white hand, symbolizing comradery between the two races.

The Watts Riot

One of the worst riots in American history oc-
curred in the Watts neighborhood of Los Angeles.
What caused the riots? How much damage was sus-
tained?

Throughout the 1940s and 1950s, the African American population of Los Angeles surged from about 63,000 to more than 350,000. This influx of population in a relatively small amount of time caused severe shortages in housing and jobs, as well as over-crowded schools and all-around poor living conditions for many.

As the African American community grew, so did the discrimination many of them faced. They were excluded from high-paying jobs, not allowed to partic-ipate in politics, and even denied affordable housing. A variety of different methods were used to prevent African Americans from moving into, or even passing through a "white neighborhood". Black motorists would frequently be pulled over for minor traffic violations or even a suspicion that a law had been violated.

The tension between the African American population and the white population in Los Angeles eventually reached its peak. The city was comparable to a keg of gunpowder... all that was necessary to ignite it, was one spark. In August of 1965, that spark occurred.

On Wednesday, August 11th, 1965, Marquette Frye, a twenty-one-year-old African American male, was pulled over by the California Highway Patrol for reckless driving. After the police officer discovered that Frye was intoxicated, he was placed under arrest. Frye's brother, Ronald, rushed to their mother's house, Rena Price, who lived only a few blocks away.

Upon the return of Price and Ronald Frye, there was an altercation between the family and the police officers at the scene. It is unclear what happened, but someone was shoved, punches were thrown, guns were drawn, and the police were required to use force to subdue the Frye brothers. Marquette and Ronald Frye, along with Rena Price, were all arrested.

During the altercation, a crowd gathered to watch the events unfold. As the arrests were being made, angry African American citizens began throwing rocks at the police officers. Word spread amongst the community that white police officers had brutalized three blacks. The crowd continued to grow and become even more agitated. More police officers arrived, attempting to disperse the mob, but this only led to more altercations. The swarm of protestors continued throwing rocks and chunks of concrete at the police.

That night, the neighborhood saw increasing discontent, and by the next day (August 12th), community leaders were calling for everyone to remain calm. This plea was not heeded. Over the next several days, the rioting became more intense. Over 900 members of the Los Angeles Police Department, more than 700 officers from the Los Angeles County Sheriff's Department, and nearly 4,000 National Guardsmen were called in to try and restore order.

It has been estimated that more than 30,000 adults actively participated at some point during the six days of rioting. During that time, police were attacked, white motorists were pulled from their vehicles and beaten, and a large number of white-owned businesses were looted. There were also countless fires started, and roads were barricaded to prevent firefighters from performing their duties.

By the time the riots reached a conclusion, more than 1,000 buildings had been destroyed, and it has been estimated that the community suffered more than $40 million in property damage. A total of 3,438 arrests were made, more than 1,000 injuries were reported, and 34 people lost their lives.

The Watts Riots have never been forgotten. There have been numerous books written about the subject, some historical, and some which are first-hand accounts of the events which unfolded. Watts has also been the subject of multiple films throughout the years.

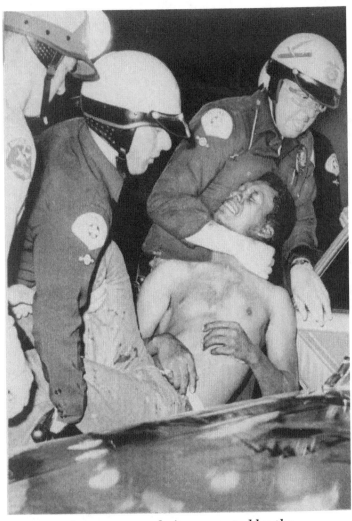

A young man being arrested by the police during the Watts Riot.

Malcolm X

During the 1960s, Malcolm X became one of the most vocal activists in the Civil Rights Movement. Who was Malcolm X? What were some of his beliefs?

Malcom X was born with the name Malcolm Little. He was born in May of 1925, in Omaha, Nebraska, one of seven children in his family. When Malcolm was only six, his father was killed by a streetcar. Even though the death was ruled an accident, there were many who believed that a group of white racists had been responsible for his father's death. This incident may have helped shape some of Malcolm's philosophies later in life.

As a boy, Malcolm hoped to become a lawyer, but was told by a white teacher that it was impractical for a black boy to dream of being a lawyer. Shortly thereafter, he dropped out of school and became involved with a life of crime. By 1943, he was living in Harlem, New York and was involved with many different illegal

Malcolm X

activities, from drug dealing to robbery. He was arrested for larceny and was sent to the Charlestown State Prison to serve out an eight-to-ten year prison sentence.

During his stay in prison, Malcolm developed a love for reading, devouring books on many different topics. Relatives began writing to him about a new religious movement known as the Nation of Islam. The Nation of Islam preached a message of black self-reliance and encouraged a return to Africa, where blacks could be free of racism.

Malcolm's interest in the Nation of Islam blossomed while he was in prison, and he gave up eating pork and smoking, both of which were against the religion's tenets. Through his indoctrination into the Nation of Islam, Malcolm came to believe that almost every association he had experienced with white individuals had been filled with deception and hatred.

While in prison, Malcolm developed a close relationship with the Nation of Islam's leader, Elijah Muhammad, who counseled him to turn away from his criminal past and stop engaging in destructive behaviors. In 1950, Malcolm began calling himself Malcolm X. He took this name because he claimed that his last name, Little, was bestowed by white slave owners who had once owned his family, and he had no desire to be associated with it. (Later in the 1950s, he also adopted the name Malcolm Shabazz, or Milek el-Shabazz, but continued to be known by the public as Malcolm X).

He was released from prison in 1952 and quickly

became one of the most active members of the Nation of Islam. He established numerous temples across the country and was largely responsible for the rapid growth of the religion throughout the latter half of the 1950s.

Malcolm X was a powerful and very influential speaker. He also possessed a physically intimidating presence. He was 6' 3", weighed 180 pounds, was quite handsome, and was always well-dressed. In many ways, this made him the ideal spokesperson for not only the Nation of Islam, but for African Americans as well.

Following the beliefs of the Nation of Islam, he encouraged Black Nationalism and argued for blacks to separate themselves from white America. As he gained prominence, his message began resonating with large numbers of African Americans. Many felt that African Americans had waited far too long for justice and equality. Malcolm seemed to articulate their frustrations better than other Civil Rights leaders.

By 1960, Malcom X was meeting with world leaders at the United Nations in New York. His quotes and comments were becoming increasingly common in newspapers and on television. The media frequently sought out his opinion because his comments were always flamboyant and controversial. He strongly disagreed with Civil Rights leaders who believed in nonviolence. Instead, he advocated that African Americans should achieve equal rights by any means available to them. Once, in 1964, he even delivered a speech titled "The Ballot or the Bullet". In this speech, he suggested that it might be necessary to take up arms to achieve full equality.

Malcolm X's message was not appreciated by everyone. Many whites and even some blacks feared that Malcolm's message of violence might ultimately harm the Civil Rights Movement and cause resentment between black and white Americans. His critics referred to him as a racist, a black supremacist, and a hate-monger.

In 1964, Malcolm X announced that he was leaving the Nation of Islam in favor of becoming a Sunni Muslim. He also retracted many of his earlier beliefs, no longer advocating separation from white America. He announced that he would try to actively work with other Civil Rights leaders towards accomplishing the goals of social and political equality.

Sadly, this newfound cooperation with other Civil Rights leaders would be short-lived. As Malcolm X was preparing to speak to the Organization for Afro-American Unity on February 21, 1965, he was gunned down by several assassins. He was shot twenty-one times in the chest, shoulder, arms, and legs. He was rushed to a hospital, but was pronounced dead at 3:30 PM. In the days leading up to his funeral, his body was viewed by no less than 14,000 people who wanted to pay their respects to the fallen Civil Rights leader.

Malcolm X is remembered today as one of the most influential African Americans in history. He has been recognized in a number of different ways. There are dozens of schools named in his honor, as well as streets in many cities across the nation. His life was also depicted in a major motion picture, *Malcolm X*, in 1992, starring Denzel Washington in the title role. Additionally, May 19th (his birthday) is honored as Malcolm X Day in several cities throughout the United States.

Black Power

In the 1960s, a philosophy known as "Black Power" emerged. What was the Black Power philosophy? Who popularized the use of this phrase?

"Black Power" was a phrase that had been in use since the 1850s. At that time, Frederick Douglass had used the phrase to describe the political power held by slave-owning Southerners. However, its more modern usage comes from the civil rights activist Stokely Carmichael.

Carmichael was one of the key figures of the Student Non-Violent Coordinating Committee, a leading civil rights group. He first used the phrase on June 16, 1966, following the shooting of James Meredith. He stated, *"The only way we gonna stop them white men from whuppin' us is to take over. What we gonna start sayin' now is Black Power!"*

Carmichael explained that his view of Black Power meant solidarity between African Americans. The use

Stokely Carmichael

of the phrase Black Power was an effort to emphasize racial pride and help establish a common cultural identity amongst African Americans.

Several different organizations adopted the Black Power philosophy, and the phrase came to mean many different things to many different people. Some advocated "black separatism". This was the notion that African Americans should work to separate themselves from white culture and start their own institutions which were not dominated by whites. Some even advocated a separate homeland for blacks.

One of the most notable demonstrations involving Black Power ideology took place at the 1968 Summer Olympics in Mexico City. Tommie Smith and John Carlos, who had won the gold and bronze medals in the 200 meter race, raised their fists in the iconic Black Power salute. The athletes were both praised and reprimanded for their actions.

There were many critics of the Black Power philosophy. Some felt that the movement was alienating African Americans from mainstream society. Others felt that some organizations that identified themselves with Black Power, such as the Black Panther Party, were far too militant and were viewed negatively by the public. Others felt that it diverted attention away from the meaningful debate over racial equality.

However, the Black Power movement was not without its positive impacts as well. It helped African Americans establish an ethnic identity and generated meaningful discussions about "what it means to be African American". It also sparked a wave of interest in African American studies in schools across the nation.

Tommie Smith and John Carlos displaying the Black Power salute at the 1968 Summer Olympics in Mexico City.

<u>*The Black Panther Party*</u>

One of the most well-known Civil Rights organizations of the late 1960s was the Black Panther Party. Who started the Black Panther Party? What did the group advocate?

In many Northern and Western cities in the US, African Americans were living in urban ghettos with high unemployment rates and substandard housing. Many also believed that they were treated unfairly and in some cases even brutalized by police forces which did not represent them. For example, Oakland, California had 661 police officers, yet only 16 of those were African American.

Huey P. Newton and Bobby Seale had been involved in many different civil rights organizations in their young lives, including those who promoted the "black power" ideology. However, they were frustrated with the failure of these organizations to combat police brutality and other injustices they saw in their communities.

In October of 1966, the two men formed the Black Panther Party for Self-Defense (later simply known as the Black Panther Party). They organized armed patrols that would follow police officers, monitoring them for incidents of abuse. If the police attempted to confront them, Black Panther members would recite the state and federal laws which permitted them to carry their loaded weapons.

The Black Panther Party first gained national attention after an incident in 1967. The group carried loaded firearms into the California State Assembly in protest of a piece of legislation which would make carrying loaded firearms illegal. Six of the members were arrested for this incident.

In May of 1967, the Black Panther Party issued a list of ten points which stated their beliefs and values. This list included things such as full employment, decent housing, and an end to police brutality. They also sought education for African Americans and justice within the court system. The group's ideals resonated within the black community, and their numbers expanded rapidly.

By 1968, the Black Panther Party had a presence in more than twenty major American cities, including New York City, Chicago, Boston, Dallas, Los Angeles, and Washington D.C. Some estimates claim that their membership numbers were as high as 10,000 at its peak in 1969.

The party also boasted an influential newspaper

Black Panther Party members

which was read by more than 250,000 people. Its editor was Eldridge Cleaver, and he became a persuasive voice within the black power movement. Cleaver would eventually become the third most prominent member of the Black Panthers, behind Newton and Seale.

The Black Panther Party also started community-friendly programs, such as the Free Breakfast for Children Program. They believed that they could provide for the needs of those in poverty better than the government could. It has been estimated that the Black Panther Party fed more than 20,000 children through this program during the 1968-69 school year. The organization offered other services as well, including clothes distribution, classes on politics and economics, free medical care, and lessons on self-defense and first aid. They also set up an ambulance program and drug rehabilitation services.

However, the Federal Bureau of Investigation did not agree with many of the organization's paramilitary activities (carrying loaded guns, etc.). The FBI regarded them as a "black nationalist hate group", and FBI Director J. Edgar Hoover even referred to them as "the greatest threat to the internal security of the country." The group was targeted for investigation with the intent of weakening the group's power and damaging their credibility.

The Black Panther Party continued to exist as an organization throughout the 1970s, but never regained the prestige that they had once enjoyed. Over the course of that decade, their numbers dwindled away until, by 1980, only 27 people were still official members of the Black Panther Party.

Shirley Chisholm

In 1968, Shirley Chisholm made history. Where did Shirley Chisholm come from? What did she do to make history?

Shirley Chisholm was born with the name Shirley Anita St. Hill. Her parents were immigrants who settled in Brooklyn, New York. Her father was from British Guiana, her mother from Barbados. When Shirley was only three, she was sent away to Barbados to live with her grandmother. Her parents desired for her to be educated there, in a British school, rather than in the American school system. As a result, Shirley spoke with a noticeable accent her entire life.

She attended high school at an integrated high school in Brooklyn and at Brooklyn College as well. After college, she met Conrad O. Chisholm and the two were married. Shirley worked as the director for Friends Day Nursery and also earned a Master's Degree in Elementary Education from Columbia Univer

Shirley Chisholm

sity.

Chisholm became interested in state politics and began volunteering with organizations such as the League of Women Voters. In 1965, Chisholm won a seat in the New York State Assembly. She served in this position until 1968 when she ran for United States Congress.

Chisholm announced her candidacy for the House of Representatives in January of 1968. In June, she defeated two other Democrats to become her party's nominee. That November, she defeated Republican James Farmer Jr. in the general election. With this victory, Shirley Chisholm became the first African American woman elected to the United States Congress.

As a member of Congress, she helped found the Congressional Black Caucus and was also one of the charter members of the National Women's Political Caucus.

On January 25, 1972, Chisholm announced that she was running for president. Unfortunately, her campaign was short lived. She received little funding and spent a mere $300,000 campaigning. She struggled to win acceptance as a legitimate candidate. In the 1972 Democrat primaries, her best finish was in North Carolina, where she finished in third place with 7.5% of the vote. In larger, more competitive states, she was unable to earn more than 4.4% of the vote.

Following the end of her career in Congress, Chisholm resumed her career as an educator. She taught a variety of classes at Mount Holyoke College. She also traveled the country and spoke at many different universities. During these speeches, she always encouraged students to avoid intolerance and accept those who were different.

Shirley Chisholm died on January 1st, 2005. She has been honored in several different ways. She was inducted into the National Women's Hall of Fame, and in 2014, the United States Postal Service issued a stamp in Chisholm's memory.

Jesse Jackson

Throughout the 1970s, '80s, and '90s, one of the most influential voices for civil rights was the Reverend Jesse Jackson. Who was Jesse Jackson? How did he become prominent in the Civil Rights Movement?

Jesse Jackson was born in 1941, in Greenville, South Carolina. At the time of Jackson's birth, his mother was 16 and his father was 33. He was a successful student in high school, serving as the student class president and playing football, baseball, and basketball. He was offered a minor league baseball contract out of high school, but turned it down for a scholarship to play college football at the University of Illinois.

After transferring to North Carolina A&T, Jackson was elected the student body president and played quarterback. While on campus, he became actively involved in the Civil Rights Movement, protesting

Jesse Jackson

against segregated restaurants, theaters, and libraries. He graduated in 1964 with a degree in sociology. He then attended the Chicago Theological Seminary, but dropped out so he could focus on the Civil Rights Movement.

He began working with Martin Luther King Jr. and participated in the Selma to Montgomery marches in 1965. King and other civil rights leaders were quickly impressed by Jackson and gave him increasing amounts of responsibility. Before long, Jackson was chosen to be the national director of the Southern Christian Leadership Conference's economic organization, known as Operation Breadbasket. Operation Breadbasket encouraged boycotts of white businesses unless they hired black workers and also encouraged African American consumers to purchase goods from black-owned businesses.

Jackson was present on April 4, 1968 when Martin Luther King Jr. was assassinated. Jackson claimed that he was the last to speak to King and held King in his arms as he died. This account has been disputed by those who were close to King, but has never fully been disproven.

Following King's death, Jesse Jackson was viewed by many as King's successor. At the time, Jackson was still one of the few black activists who was still preaching King's message of racial harmony (many others had adopted the "black power" philosophy). Jackson also hoped to focus more on economic and class issues, rather than just race.

In 1971, Jackson formed People United to Save Humanity (later known as People United to Serve Humanity), or Operation PUSH. This organization would work to pressure politicians into improving economic opportunities for people of all races. Jackson also organized the Rainbow Coalition in 1984. This was an organization that sought to bring African Americans together with Asian Americans, Arab Americans, veterans, farmers, homosexuals, and Jews for the political purpose of helping the disadvantaged.

Jackson announced he would seek the presidency in the 1984 presidential election. This represented the first legitimate effort by an African American to run a national presidential campaign. He finished third in the Democrat primaries, behind Gary Hart and the eventual nominee Walter Mondale. Jackson sought the presidency again in 1988. In that election, he was briefly regarded as the frontrunner in the Democrat primaries, before losing out to Michael Dukakis.

In August of 2000, President Bill Clinton awarded Jesse Jackson with the Presidential Medal of Freedom for his lifetime of work in the field of civil rights. This is the highest honor that the nation can award to a civilian. In 2002, he was named amongst the 100 Greatest African Americans.

Colin Powell

One of the most prominent generals of the 1990s was Colin Powell. Who was Powell? How did he rise to such an important level?

Colin Powell was born in Harlem on April 5th, 1937. He was raised in the South Bronx, where he graduated from Morris High School in 1954. He attended City College of New York where he earned a degree in geology. While in college, he also joined the Reserve Officers' Training Corps (ROTC). Upon graduating, he became a second lieutenant in the US Army and was sent to basic training at Fort Benning, Georgia.

In 1962, Powell traveled to Vietnam and served as an advisor to the South Vietnamese Army. He returned to Vietnam in 1968 during a second tour of duty. While there, he survived a helicopter crash and single-handedly rescued three others from the wreckage, including his division commander.

Powell steadily rose through the ranks, working

Colin Powell

with both the Nixon administration and the Reagan administration. In the early 1980s, Powell was named the senior military assistant to Secretary of Defense Casper Weinberger. In 1987, at the age of 49, Powell became the National Security Advisor for Ronald Reagan. He was the first African American to ever hold this position.

General Powell earned his fourth star in 1989. He served as the Commander in Chief, Forces Command. This meant that he oversaw all US Army, US Army Reserve, and National Guard troops in the continental United States, Alaska, Hawaii, and Puerto Rico.

At the Age of 52, Powell was selected by President George H. W. Bush to be the Chairman of the Joint Chiefs of Staff. This is the highest military position in the Department of Defense. He was the youngest general to ever hold this title and also the only African American to ever do so.

While he was Chairman of the Joint Chiefs of Staff, he oversaw the invasion of Panama to remove Manuel Noriega from power, as well as Operation Desert Storm in 1991. He held this position through the remainder of Bush's presidency and even into the Clinton administration. However, he eventually resigned due to disagreements with the Clinton administration over foreign policy issues.

In 2000, after George W. Bush won the presidency, Powell was called upon again to serve his nation. As the first African American to hold the role of Secretary of State, Powell played a critical role in the days following the World Trade Center attack on September 11th, 2001 and helped initiate the global War on Terrorism.

Powell has received numerous awards throughout his life, both military and civilian. He has won the Presidential Medal of Freedom twice, as well as the President's Citizens Medal. He has also received the Congressional Gold Medal, the Secretary of State Distinguished Service Medal, and the Ronald Reagan Freedom Award. He has also had several schools named in his honor.

Barack Obama

In 2008, Barack Obama became the first African American President of the United States. What did Barack Obama do before he became president? How did he achieve that position?

Barack Hussein Obama was born in Honolulu, Hawaii on August 4th, 1961. His father was from Kenya while his mother was a white woman from Wichita, Kansas.

After high school, Obama attended Occidental College in Los Angeles, starting in 1979. Two years later, he transferred to Columbia University in New York City. He graduated from Columbia in 1983 with a degree in political science. He worked for a brief time with the Business International Corporation and the New York Public Interest Research Group.

In 1985, Obama was hired as the director of the Developing Communities Project. In this role, he helped establish a college preparatory tutoring program, a

jobs training program, and a tenants' rights organization.

In 1988, Obama enrolled at Harvard Law School
where he served as the editor for the *Harvard Law
Review*. The next year, he became the president of
that journal, the first African American to hold this
position. After graduating from Harvard in 1991, he
signed a publishing contract for a book which would
eventually be titled *Dreams from My Father*, which
was published in 1995.

Obama was hired to teach constitutional law at the
University of Chicago Law School. He held this position for twelve years, from 1992 to 2004. During that
time, he also directed Project Vote, a voter registration
campaign which succeeded in registering more than
150,000 African Americans to vote.

In 1996, Obama was elected to the Illinois Senate.
He was re-elected in both 1998 and 2002 (in 2000 he
left the seat in an unsuccessful bid for a seat in the US
House of Representatives). In 2004, Obama delivered
the keynote address at the 2004 Democratic National
Convention. This speech was well-received and pro-
pelled Obama onto the national stage. That same year
he was elected to the United States Senate, winning
70% of the vote.

In February of 2007, Barack Obama announced his
candidacy for President of the United States. He won
a hard-fought primary election against former First
Lady Hillary Clinton to become the Democrat nominee. In the general election, he was matched against

Barack Obama

the Republican candidate, John McCain. He defeated McCain, winning 365 electoral votes to McCain's 173. He also won 52.9% of the popular vote. With this election, Obama became the first African American elected president.

In 2009, Obama was awarded the Nobel Peace Prize for his "extraordinary efforts to strengthen international diplomacy and cooperation between peoples". He was only the fourth American president to win the award.

Obama was re-elected to the presidency in 2012, once again winning by a sizeable majority. In the 2012 election, he received 51.1% of the popular vote, making him the first Democrat since Franklin Roosevelt to win a majority of the popular vote in two elections.

Motown

One of the most successful record companies of all-time is the legendary Motown. How did Motown get its start? How did it become so successful?

In the late 1950s, Berry Gordy was working as a struggling song writer. He had written popular songs for performers such as The Matadors and Jack Wilson, but he felt that he was not earning as much money as he should. He became aware that if he truly wanted to succeed in the music business, he needed to own his own company that produced records and published music.

He made the decision to borrow $800 from family members, and on January 12, 1959, he founded a record company in Detroit known as Tamla Records. The record company started experiencing some local success in the Detroit area and had its first hit with "Money (That's What I Want)", which rose to #2 on Billboard magazine's R&B charts.

Tamla Records eventually changed its name to Motown. The company signed an up-and-coming group known as The Miracles. Their lead singer was William "Smokey" Robinson. Robinson became one of the most popular singing acts of the 1960s. He also proved to be a prolific songwriter, writing songs not only for himself but for other Motown performers as well. "Shop Around", "The Way You Do the Things You Do", "My Girl", "I Second that Emotion", and "The Tears of a Clown" were all written by Robinson, amongst many, many others. Robinson would eventually become the vice-president of the company.

"Shop Around" became Motown's first single to sell more than one million copies. The next year, "Please Mr. Postman" by the Marvelettes became the company's first song to reach #1 on the Billboard Hot 100.

In 1959, Motown started in a single, tiny recording studio (which the Gordy family lived in a small apartment above). By 1966, the company had 450 employees and a gross income of more than $20 million. During the 1960s, Motown produced 110 "top ten" songs. Many different artists worked with the company, including The Supremes, The Four Tops, The Jackson Five, Stevie Wonder, Marvin Gaye, Gladys Knight, and The Temptations, just to name a few.

As Motown continued to grow, they expanded their operation into New York and Los Angeles. They also established Motown Productions, which produced television specials for various Motown performers.

"Hitsville USA" was the headquarters for Motown from 1959 to 1968. Today it serves as a museum for the historic recording company.

The Apollo Theater

One of New York City's legendary venues is the Apollo Theater. Why did the Apollo become so well-known? How long has it been around?

In 1913-14, a building was constructed in Harlem that would house the Hurtig and Seamon's New Theater. This was a "whites-only" establishment that specialized in burlesque productions. The theater closed and fell into disrepair during the early 1930s, but was purchased by new owners in 1933. The new owner, Sidney Cohen, refurbished the theater and reopened the facility as the Apollo Theater on January 16, 1934. The Apollo quickly developed a reputation as a stand-out venue for African American performers.

Early Apollo shows were similar to vaudeville performances, with a dancing chorus line, musical acts, comedy routines, and other types of entertainment. In the 1940s, some of the biggest names in swing music performed at the Apollo, including Duke Ellington,

*The historic sign which hangs outs
ide the Apollo Theater*

Dizzy Gillespie, and Count Basie. Over the years, countless notable singers have performed at the Apollo, including Sam Cooke, Ray Charles, Otis Redding, Aretha Franklin, and many others.

The Apollo Theater became well-known for its famous "Amateur Night in Harlem", which was held every Monday night and broadcast over the radio. This was a night when amateurs could perform in front of the Apollo audience and attempt to win the weekly prize. Famous singer Ella Fitzgerald made her debut as a performer on "Amateur Night", winning the $25 prize for first place. Many years later, a young guitar player named Jimi Hendrix also won first prize on "Amateur Night".

Billie Holiday, Sammy Davis Jr., James Brown, Diana Ross, Gladys Knight, Stevie Wonder, Ben E. King, and Luther Vandross are just a few of the people who also got their start at the Apollo Theater. Many comedians have also begun their careers in the Apollo. Redd Foxx, Bill Cosby, and Richard Pryor all performed in the theater.

While the Apollo became well-known for highlighting African American talent, several white performers played the Apollo as well. Additionally, the Apollo's audience was made up of both races. It has been estimated that during the 1940s, the average Apollo show was approximately 40% white. This type of integrated setting would have been very unusual for a theater at that time.

The Apollo experienced its most successful decade

in the 1960s. In 1962, James Brown recorded an album, *Live at the Apollo*, which became a huge success. This album stayed on the popular music charts for 66 weeks.

As the neighborhood of Harlem declined in the 1970s, the Apollo declined as well. The theater was closed in 1976 after an 8-year-old boy was shot to death. However, the theater was restored and reopened later that same year.

Today, the Apollo Theater is regarded as a historic landmark, and both the exterior and interior of the building have been restored. The theater celebrated its 80th Anniversary in 2014-15. It has been estimated that the Apollo receives 1.3 million visitors each year.

Roots

One of the most viewed television events of all-time was the miniseries Roots. What was Roots about? Were there any notable actors in the series?

In October of 1976, a novel titled *Roots* was first published. Author Alex Haley had written the book, loosely based on his ancestors' journey from Africa to America and beyond. The story begins with a young Mandinka warrior, Kunta Kinte. At the age of 15, Kunta is training to become a man when he is kidnapped by slave hunters and taken on a boat to America.

The novel follows Kunta throughout his life as he adjusts to his role as a slave. The story continues through several generations of the family, taking the narrative up through the Civil War.

Upon its release, *Roots* was instantly popular. It debuted at #5 on the New York Times Best Seller list. In just over a month, it had moved to the #1 spot. It stayed on the bestseller list for 22 weeks and sold more than 1.5 million copies in seven months.

Plans were immediately made to turn the novel into a television adaptation. The miniseries *Roots* aired in January of 1977. It featured Levar Burton as the teenage Kunta Kinte and John Amos as the adult Kunta Kinte.

Many other notable African American actors of the era appeared in the drama. Lou Gossett Jr., Ben Vereen, Scatman Crothers, Maya Angelou, and O.J. Simpson all had roles, to name just a few. Several famous white actors also appeared, including Ed Asner, Robert Reed, Chuck Conners, Sandy Duncan, Lloyd Bridges, Lorne Greene, Burl Ives, and a host of others.

The miniseries became incredibly popular. It aired over eight consecutive evenings (January 23rd through January 30th) and gained a significant amount of viewership each night. It has been estimated that approximately 80 million people viewed *Roots* each night that it aired. The final episode was watched by more than 100 million! It was speculated that roughly 140 million viewers watched at least one episode of the program. At the time, the population of the United States was 220 million. This means that over 60% of the population was watching *Roots* at some point that week. The final episode is the third most watched episode for a program in the history of television.

Roots was critically acclaimed as well. The series was nominated for a spectacular thirty-seven Emmy Awards, winning in nine of those categories. Amongst the Emmy's it was awarded were Best Director and

Best Actor. *Roots* also received the Golden Globe Award for Best Dramatic TV Series.

Roots had a profound impact on the American culture. Many African Americans became interested in tracing their family's history back to its tribal roots. The series also caused an increased awareness in African American history.

Maya Angelou

Maya Angelou became one of the most famous African American women of the latter half of the 20ᵗʰ Century. Why was Angelou so famous? How has she been honored?

Maya Angelou was born with the name Marguerite Annie Johnson, on April 4, 1928, in St. Louis, Missouri. She acquired the nickname "Maya" from an older brother. At an early age, Maya went to live with her grandmother, who ran a general store in Stamps, Arkansas.

Maya's young life was tumultuous. She was abused by her mother's boyfriend, who was later killed by her relatives for his actions. This incident left Maya mute for nearly five years. During her years of silence, she developed a love for reading.

As a teenager, Maya moved to Oakland, California where she attended the California Labor School. She worked as San Francisco's first African American streetcar conductor. At the age of 17, she gave birth to a son.

In the 1950s, Maya enjoyed a career as a dancer. She danced and sang professionally to calypso music, which was very popular at the time. A manager of one of the establishments she performed at suggested that she change her name. Up to that point, she had been performing as Marguerite Johnson. She chose the professional name Maya Angelou because she felt it captured the spirit of her calypso dancing.

Angelou traveled Europe and performed in stage productions. Along the way, she became proficient in many different languages. In 1957, Angelou recorded her first album, *Miss Calypso*. She also participated in an off-Broadway production in which she sang and performed her own songs.

In the early 1960s, Angelou became involved in the Civil Rights Movement. She was appointed as the Southern Christian Leadership Conference's Northern Coordinator.

She moved to Cairo, Egypt and worked as the associate editor for an English-language newspaper. Not long after that, she moved to Ghana where she served as an administrator for the University of Ghana and worked as a broadcaster for Radio Ghana. While living in Ghana, she became close friends with Malcolm X and returned to the United States to help him build the Organization of Afro-American Unity.

Following Malcolm X's assassination, Angelou moved to Los Angeles to focus on her writing career.

Maya Angelou

She wrote, produced, and narrated a ten part documentary, *Blacks, Blues, Black!,* for National Education Television. She also wrote her first autobiography in 1969 titled *I Know Why the Caged Bird Sings*.

Georgia, Georgia was a film written by Maya Angelou. It was produced in Sweden and became the first screenplay written by an African American woman to be made into a movie. She also wrote the music for the film.

Throughout the 1970s, Angelou became a prolific author. She wrote screenplays, articles, short stories, documentaries, TV scripts, autobiographies, poetry, and even composed music scores. She was a successful actress as well. She performed on stage, winning a Tony Award for her role in 1973's *Look Away*. She also acted on TV, appearing in a small role in the television miniseries *Roots*.

Despite having never gone to college, Angelou became a professor at Wake Forest University, where she taught philosophy, ethics, theology, theater, and writing. In 1993, she was asked to recite her poem "On the Pulse of Morning" at the inauguration of President Bill Clinton. This led to increased recognition and a renewed interest in her work. She eventually won a Grammy Award for her recitation of this poem.

In 1996, Angelou achieved a long-time goal. She directed a feature film, *Down in the Delta*. This was the first major motion picture to be directed by an African American woman.

Throughout her life, Maya Angelou wrote seven autobiographies, as well as several volumes of poetry, seven children's books, numerous screenplays for both film and television, and even two cookbooks! She was awarded a Tony Award, three Grammy Awards, was nominated for a Pulitzer Prize, and was given more than 50 honorary degrees by various universities across the nation.

Angelou died on May 28, 2014. A memorial service was held for her, which included speeches from First Lady Michelle Obama, Oprah Winfrey, and former president Bill Clinton. In 2015, the United States Postal Service honored Maya Angelou with a commemorative stamp.

<u>*Michael Jackson*</u>

One of the most legendary entertainers of all-time was Michael Jackson. What kind of entertainment was Michael Jackson famous for? How successful did he become?

Michael Jackson was born in Gary, Indiana on August 29, 1958. He was the eighth of what would eventually be ten children born into the Jackson family. They lived in a two-bedroom home, and his parents struggled to provide for their children.

In 1965, Michael began performing with his brothers, in a musical group that became known as the Jackson Five. After winning a local talent show, the brothers began performing at black night clubs, school dances, and local auditoriums. During that time, the group opened for other famous performers such as Gladys Knight and Etta James.

In 1969, the Jackson Five signed a contract with Motown. Michael quickly emerged as the group's star, singing lead vocals. The group's first four singles, including "I'll Be There" and "ABC", all reached number one on the pop music charts.

In the mid-1970s, Jackson began to establish himself as a solo performer, slowly separating from his brothers. He released four solo albums throughout the 1970s, but it was not until his 1979 album, *Off the Wall*, that he truly broke through as a solo artist. This album sold more than 20 million copies worldwide.

Jackson experienced unprecedented success in the early 1980s. His album, *Thriller*, became the best-selling album of all time in the United States, as well as the best-selling album of all time worldwide. It produced seven top ten singles including "Billie Jean", "Beat It", and of course, "Thriller". The album stayed at number one on the sales charts for 37 weeks and remained in the top ten for 80 weeks. It eventually sold more than 65 million copies.

During this time period, Jackson also became known for eccentric dressing style, as well as his prolific dancing ability. His trademark fashion style became a single white glove decorated in rhinestones. His signature dance move became the "moonwalk", which he debuted in 1983 on a special television appearance watched by an estimated 47 million viewers.

Other successful albums followed, and Michael Jackson became a household name. He became known as "the King of Pop" (referring to "popular music"). In 1989, Jackson went on a world tour which smashed records of all varieties. In Japan alone, he

Michael Jackson in 1984

drew 570,000 fans to 14 sellout performances. Another 500,000 came to seven sold-out shows at Wembley Stadium in London. Throughout the tour, he performed a total of 123 concerts in front of 4.4 million people.

Jackson became unbelievably wealthy through album sales, as well as other lucrative endorsements. It has been estimated that Jackson earned more than $750 million throughout his life. He was also recognized many times by the music industry for his abilities. He was awarded thirteen Grammy Awards and twenty-six American Music Awards. He has a star on the Hollywood Walk of Fame and has been inducted into the Rock n' Roll Hall of Fame twice (once as a member of the Jackson Five and again as a solo performer).

Michael Jackson died on June 25th, 2009. The cause of death was generally attributed to a dangerous mix of prescription medications. Jackson's death caused an outpouring of grief around the world. His memorial service was streamed online and viewed by an estimated 31 million people.

<u>*Oprah Winfrey*</u>

One of the most prominent African American women in recent history has been Oprah Winfrey. Where did Oprah Winfrey come from? How did she become so successful?

Oprah Winfrey was born in 1954, in Kosciusko, Mississippi. Her mother worked as a housemaid throughout most of her life and was a teenager at the time of Oprah's birth. Oprah lived the first six years of her life with her grandmother who taught her to read. The family was very poor, and Oprah even wore dresses made from potato sacks.

Winfrey spent time throughout her childhood living with both her mother in Milwaukee, Wisconsin and her father in Nashville, Tennessee. When she was thirteen, she ran away from home and gave birth to a child at the age of fourteen (which was born prematurely and died not long after birth).

As Winfrey grew older, she began to take her school

career more seriously. While attending East Nashville High School, she became an honors student, joined her high school debate team, and was voted Most Popular Girl. When she was seventeen, she won the Miss Black Tennessee beauty pageant as well as a speech contest which helped her earn a scholarship to Tennessee State University.

Winfrey became involved in broadcasting at a young age. She was hired by a radio station, WVOL, to read news during her senior year in high school. She maintained this position throughout the first two years of college. After graduating from college, she became the first African American news anchor on Nashville's WLAC-TV. In 1976, she relocated to Baltimore, where she worked as a news anchor and hosted a local talk show.

Oprah Winfrey

In 1984, Winfrey began hosting a morning television talk show in Chicago, titled *AM Chicago*. In only two months, the show had become the highest rated talk show in the Chicago market. The program was retitled *The Oprah Winfrey Show* and began to broadcast nationally on September 8th, 1986. It quickly became the most watched daytime talk show in America, drawing more than twice the number of viewers as the second-rated program.

Aside from her success with *The Oprah Winfrey Show*, Oprah expanded into other genres of media as well. In 1985, she co-starred in the film *The Color Purple*, for which she received an Academy Award nomination for Best Supporting Actress. Winfrey also produced and starred in the 1989 miniseries *The Women of Brewster Place*. In addition to these endeavors, she has also founded two television networks, Oxygen (a network devoted to women's programming) and OWN: Oprah Winfrey Network. She also established Harpo Productions, a production company which specializes in producing television programming for women.

Oprah Winfrey became a millionaire at the age of 32. By the age of 41, she was worth over $300 million. By the year 2000, her net worth was approximately $800 million, and she was believed to have been the wealthiest African American of the 20th Century. In 2008, it was estimated that her yearly income was $275 million. From 2004 to 2006, Forbes Magazine claimed that Winfrey was the only African American billionaire, and she became the first black female billionaire in the history of the world.

She has been referred to as "the most powerful woman in the world" and the "most influential woman in the world" by various publications. TIME magazine included her amongst the "100 people who most influenced the 20th Century," and Life magazine named her as part of its "100 people who changed the world."

The Harlem Globetrotters

For more than eighty years, the entire world has been entertained by the antics of the Harlem Globe-trotters. Who are the Harlem Globetrotters? How did they become so well-known?

In November of 1927, on the south side of Chicago, Illinois, the Savoy Ballroom opened. One of the establishment's prime attractions was the Savoy Five, an exhibition basketball team. This team eventually changed its name to the Globetrotters, and they began touring throughout Illinois. The team's owner, Abe Saperstein, also decided to add the name "Harlem" to the team as a way of indicating that the players were African American. Even though the team was not actually from Harlem, it was chosen because Harlem was the center of African American culture at the time.

There were many African American players who got their start in professional basketball by playing for the Globetrotters, including Wilt Chamberlain. At the time, the Globetrotters was one of the few opportuni-

This image shows Wilt Chamberlain posing in a Harlem Globetrotters uniform.

ties for black basketball players. The National Basketball Association began play in 1946, but did not allow African American players until 1950.

The Globetrotters participated in international basketball tournaments around the world, including the World Professional Basketball Tournament, which they won in 1940. The Globetrotters even played a series of nine games in Moscow. More than 14,000 Russians watched each game.

As the Globetrotters progressed, they became known more as an exhibition team, rather than a serious basketball team. The Globetrotters are well-known for their amazing ball-handling ability, such as dribbling two balls at once, juggling basketballs, spinning the balls on their finger, or elaborate passes from one player to another.

The Harlem Globetrotters claim to have won more than 20,000 games. Most of these wins have come against their standard opponent, the Washington Generals. The Generals travel with the Globetrotters and serve as their adversary in most of their exhibition basketball games.

The Globetrotters have been featured in a film, *The Harlem Globetrotters* (1951), and have also even had their own Saturday morning cartoon show.

Muhammad Ali

Muhammad Ali is often thought of as the greatest heavyweight boxer who has ever lived. How did he earn his reputation as such a great fighter? Did he do anything else to earn recognition throughout his life?

On January 17th, 1942, Muhammad Ali was born with the name Cassius Clay. He was one of six children born into a middleclass family in Louisville, Kentucky. At the age of twelve, Cassius had his bike stolen. He was upset over the incident and told a Louisville police officer that he wanted to beat up the person who stole it. The officer suggested that he needed to learn how to box.

Cassius took the man's advice, and over the next several years proceeded to win several amateur championships, including an appearance in Rome at the 1960 Olympics. He won the gold medal in the light heavyweight division. He later claimed that he threw this gold medal into the Ohio River in protest of racial

Muhammad Ali

segregation. However, this claim has been debated for many years.

Clay became a professional boxer later that same year, in October of 1960. He won his first professional match in six rounds and went on to win thirty-one bouts in a row. By late 1963, Clay was considered the top contender to challenge reigning heavyweight champion Sonny Liston, which he did on February 25, 1964. Liston was heavily-favored, but the faster and more athletic Clay made Liston appear slow and awkward by comparison. The two brawled for six rounds before Clay was declared the winner by technical knockout (TKO).

Not long after this victory, Cassius Clay changed his name to Muhammad Ali. He did so after converting to Islam. He had been actively attending meetings of the Nation of Islam since 1961. Following his name change, many sports journalists (and fans) refused to refer to him by the new name. However, prominent supporters such as famous broadcaster Howard Cosell helped solidify the new name in the public consciousness.

Muhammad Ali's career as a boxer is nearly unrivaled. Throughout the 1960s and 1970s, he participated in many high-profile title defenses. Amongst the most famous were a series of three bouts against Joe Frazier. The first of these fights, on March 8, 1971, has been called "The Fight of the Century". Frazier won this bout by a unanimous decision. It was the first loss of Ali's career. Ali went on to defeat Frazier in their second and third matches. The third contest was a grueling fourteen round match in the Philippines which was titled "The Thrilla' in Manila".

Other notable bouts included a title fight between Ali and George Foreman which became known as the "Rumble in the Jungle" (because the match was fought in Zaire) and three matches against Ken Norton. Norton managed to break Ali's jaw in the first of these fights.

As a boxer, Muhammad Ali became well-known for many different things. He pioneered an unconventional strategy that became known as the "rope-a-dope" strategy. This involved allowing an opponent to throw as many punches as they could, exhausting themselves in the process. Then, once the other fighter was exhausted, Ali would go on the offensive. He would also frequently taunt his opponents before and during the match, causing them to become angry and lose focus. He was not afraid to boast of his own abilities either. He claimed he could "float like a butterfly and sting like a bee" and once famously declared, "I am the greatest!" He was a very charismatic and flamboyant fighter who was both loved and hated by boxing fans.

Muhammad Ali was not just a boxer. Throughout the 1960s and 70s, he also became an outspoken activist for various causes. He became one of the most visible members of the Nation of Islam, a religious movement made up largely of African Americans (Ali later converted to Sunni Islam). These devout religious beliefs led to one of Ali's most controversial moments.

In 1966, Ali was drafted into the United States Army. He refused to be drafted, stating that his religious beliefs forbade his participation in the war. Someone who refuses to participate in a war based on their religious beliefs is known as a conscientious objector. He was arrested and could have potentially faced a $10,000 fine and up to five years in prison. He was found guilty of the charges against him, but this conviction was eventually overturned by the U.S. Supreme Court, and Ali never served any prison time.

Unfortunately, Ali's boxing career suffered as a result. He was stripped of his heavyweight title and was denied a license to box in all fifty states. As a result, Ali was not allowed to box from March of 1967 to October of 1970. Ali's outspoken opposition to the Vietnam Conflict had a significant impact outside the boxing ring, though. Many others began to have the courage to voice their disapproval of the war. By the early 1970s, the conflict had become quite unpopular in the public eye.

In 1984, Ali was diagnosed with Parkinson's syndrome. This is a syndrome characterized by trembling and lack of physical mobility. The head trauma that he had endured from the many years of boxing had almost certainly contributed to this condition. Throughout the latter part of the 1900s, Ali's health only continued to deteriorate.

Muhammad Ali will always be remembered as one

of the greatest athletes of all time. He remains the only boxer to ever win the heavyweight championship on three separate occasions. He appeared on the cover of *Sports Illustrated* thirty-seven times, and at one time, 97% of Americans could visually recognize him. He has been the subject of countless books and several movies. More importantly perhaps, Ali has inspired countless Americans to hold true to their convictions and stand up for what they believe in.

<u>*Michael Jordan*</u>

Many people regard Michael Jordan as the greatest basketball player who has ever lived. Where did Michael Jordan come from? How did he become so legendary?

Michael Jordan was born in 1963, in Brooklyn, New York. However, when Michael was still very young, his family moved to Wilmington, North Carolina. In high school, Jordan not only played basketball, but football and baseball as well. As a basketball player, his senior year in high school he averaged 29 points, 11 rebounds, and 10 assists per game.

Jordan attended North Carolina University where he became the Freshman of the Year and made a game-winning shot in the 1982 National Championship game. After three years at North Carolina, he was the third player selected in the 1984 NBA draft, behind Hakeem Olajuwon and Sam Bowie.

In his first season with the Chicago Bulls, Jordan

averaged 28 points per game. He was voted to play in the All-Star game and won Rookie of the Year. He quickly became a fan favorite and one of the most visible stars of the league.

In the 1986-87 season, Jordan became only the second player in the history of the NBA to score 3,000 points in a single season (the first being Wilt Chamberlain). That season, he also registered 200 steals and 100 blocked shots. No player had ever accomplished this feat before.

Jordan and the Chicago Bulls won their first NBA championship in 1991 against the Los Angeles Lakers. Jordan was named the Most Valuable Player (MVP) of the championship series, averaging more than 31 points per game.

In a surprise move, in October of 1993, Michael Jordan announced his retirement from basketball. After retiring, he attempted a brief baseball career, signing with the Chicago White Sox. He played for the White Sox's minor league club, the Birmingham Barons, where he hit three home runs and had 30 stolen bases.

Jordan made the decision to return to professional basketball in March of 1995. He returned to the Chicago Bulls, temporarily wearing jersey number 45 (his traditional number of 23 had already been retired by the Bulls). In his first full season back (1995-96), the Chicago Bulls posted a staggering record of 72-10. This is the best regular season record by any team in NBA history. The team won the NBA championship

Michael Jordan

that season, and Jordan won the league's MVP award.

Michael Jordan retired for a second time on January 13, 1999. The next year, he became part owner of, and President of Basketball Operations, for the Washington Wizards. However, Jordan's desire to return to basketball proved to be overwhelming. He once again came out of retirement, this time playing for the Wizards. Even at the age of 38, he led his team in scoring with 22 points per game. Jordan's final game came on April 16, 2003.

After his retirement, Michael Jordan became part-owner of the Charlotte Bobcats. In 2010, he became the majority owner of that franchise, making him the first former player to become the majority owner of an NBA team.

Throughout his career, Michael Jordan was known for his successful business ventures. He became a recognizable spokesman for Nike, McDonalds, Gatorade, Coca-Cola, and many other major corporations. His lucrative endorsement deals, along with his NBA contracts, allowed Jordan to become the first NBA player to become a billionaire.

Michael Jordan scored 32,292 points during his regular season NBA career and an additional 5,987 points in the playoffs. He was voted the league's MVP five times and the championship series MVP six times. He was a fourteen time all-star, and he led the league in scoring during ten different seasons. The Chicago Bulls won six NBA championships with Jordan as a member of the team.

Jordan appeared on the cover of *Sports Illustrated* magazine fifty times. This is more than any other sports figure in history. He is regarded by most as the greatest player in NBA History. Not only that, but he is frequently named with Babe Ruth and Muhammad Ali as one of the greatest athletes who has ever lived.

Notable Tennis Greats

In the modern era of professional tennis, there have been three African American players who have stood out amongst the very best. Who were these three tennis players? How successful were they?

Arthur Ashe started playing tennis when he was seven years old. It instantly became apparent that he had a profound natural talent for the sport. He attended UCLA on a tennis scholarship in 1963 and was selected for the United States Davis Cup team that same year. He was the first African American selected to play in the Davis Cup for the US.

In 1968, Ashe won the United States Amateur Championships and the U.S. Open. That year, he became the number one ranked tennis player in the world. Ashe went on to win the Australian Open in 1970 and Wimbledon in 1975. He is the only African American male to win the U.S. Open, the Australian Open, and Wimbledon.

Arthur Ashe

Ashe retired from tennis in 1980. Following his retirement, he became a writer for *Time Magazine* and the *Washington Post*. He also worked as an announcer for ABC Sports, and he founded the National Junior Tennis League. Throughout his life, he was also a vocal activist for the cause of civil rights and better treatment of blacks, not just in America, but around the world.

In 1992, Ashe was diagnosed with HIV. It is believed he contracted the disease through a blood transfusion he had received in the early 1980s. He worked the rest of his life to increase public awareness about HIV and AIDS. He died on February 6, 1993, due to pneumonia. On June 20, 1993, President Bill Clinton posthumously awarded Arthur Ashe with the Presidential Medal of Freedom.

In 2005, the United States Postal Service honored Arthur Ashe by featuring him on a postage stamp. ESPN has also honored Ashe by naming an award in his honor. Each year, the television network awards the Arthur Ashe for Courage Award. This is given to a member of the sports community who displays courage in the face of adversity.

Venus Williams became the number one ranked female tennis player in the world on February 25, 2002. She was the first African American woman to be ranked number one in the modern era of tennis. She has held the number one ranking on three separate occasions.

Venus has won the Wimbledon tennis tournament

five times. This ties her for eighth place on the all-time list for Wimbledon titles. She has also won four Olympic gold medals, one as a singles player, and the other three in women's doubles, which she won with her sister, Serena.

Serena Williams is regarded by some as the greatest female tennis player of all time. She has been ranked the number one player in the world on six separate occasions. She has won more than twenty Grand Slam titles, including the U.S. Open six times, the French Open three times, the Australian Open five times, and Wimbledon seven times.

Serena and Venus Williams have also combined for thirteen titles in major tennis tournaments as doubles partners. This includes an impressive five wins at Wimbledon.

Tiger Woods

One of the greatest golfers to ever play the game is Tiger Woods. How did Tiger become so legendary? How much money did he earn?

Eldrick "Tiger" Woods was born in 1975 in southern California. His father introduced Tiger to golf before the age of two. The young prodigy displayed a natural talent for the sport, and by the age of five, he had appeared in *Golf Digest*. He won the U.S. Junior Amateur Tournament at the age of fifteen, making him the youngest golfer to ever win that tournament. He is the only golfer to win the U.S. Junior Amateur three times. In 1994, he also won the U.S. Amateur Championship, becoming the youngest golfer to win that tournament as well.

Woods attended Stanford University on a golf scholarship, but only played two seasons collegiately. He played his first professional tournaments in 1996. That year, he was named the Professional Golf Associ

Tiger Woods

ation (PGA) Rookie of the Year as well as *Sports Illustrated* magazine's Sportsman of the Year. In April of 1997, Woods won the Masters Tournament. At the age of twenty-one, he was the youngest player to ever win the tournament, as well as the first non-white player to win. Two months later, he was ranked the number one player in the world. This set a record for the fastest rise to the number one ranking.

In the year 2000, Woods won nine PGA tour events, including three "majors". At the age of twenty-four, Woods was the youngest player to achieve the "career grand slam". This means that he had won all four of the major golf tournaments (the four tournaments being the U.S. Open, The Masters, the British Open, and the PGA Championship). That year, he was once again named *Sports Illustrated*'s Sportsman of the Year. He is the only athlete to ever hold this honor twice.

Woods' achievements on the golf course brought about financial success as well. He signed lucrative endorsement contracts with Titleist, General Motors, American Express, Nike, and Gatorade. In between 1996 and 2007, Woods earned an estimated $769 million. In 2009, Woods became the first athlete in the world to earn more than a billion dollars. At the time, he was the second wealthiest African American on the planet, behind only Oprah Winfrey.

As of 2015, Woods has won seventy-nine PGA Tour events. He has won the PGA Championship four times, the Masters four times, the British Open three times, and the U.S. Open three times, for a total of fourteen major tournament wins. He was named the Male Athlete of the Year four times by the Associated Press and was also named the Associated Press Athlete of the Decade for the 2000s.

About the Author:

Jake Henderson is a graduate of Southwestern Oklahoma State University in Weatherford, OK, where he earned a BA in History Education. He also has a Master's Degree in History Education from SWOSU, which he earned in 2004. He has taught US History, World History, AP Government, US Government, Geography, Oklahoma History, and Psychology at the High School level for more than fifteen years. He currently lives and teaches in Woodward, OK.

Made in the USA
Columbia, SC
04 May 2020

95775778R00163